Jumping

from

A to Z

Teach Your Dog to Soar

M. Christine Zink D.V.M., Ph.D.

Julie Daniels

Canine Sports Productions
Lutherville, MD

Published by: Canine Sports Productions
                  1810A York Road # 360
                  Lutherville, MD. 21093

ISBN 1-888119-00-4

Cover Design by Cynthia Gillette-Fox, Ph.D., Westport, CT.
Book Design by Penny Winegartner, Lickety Split Graphics, Houston, TX.
Printing by Royal Fireworks Printing, Unionville, NY.

Limits of Liability and Disclaimer of Warranty:

The authors and publisher shall not be liable in the event of incidental or consequential damages in connection with, or arising out of, the furnishing, performance, or use of the instructions and suggestions contained in this book.

Books are available at special discounts for bulk purchases for sales promotions, fund raising, or educational use. For details contact:

Canine Sports Productions
1810A York Road # 360
Lutherville, MD. 21093
(410)561-1555

Printed in the United States of America.

DEDICATION

To Shauna, Cajun, Bannor, Tally, and Stripe —
my patient teachers.

&

To Dick and Heather —
always ready to read, listen, and help.

Acknowledgments

No book is written without the assistance of many behind-the-scene helpers. We would like to thank the dozens of people over the years who assisted in the development of this book by sharing their ideas and their observations of dogs. We also would like to acknowledge all of the dogs who gave of their patience, effort, and bodies to our research. They let us poke, prod, measure, video, and experiment with them endlessly. We are grateful to the many owners and interested human helpmates as well, especially the dedicated and beloved group from NEAT. Special thanks, as always, to our personal sounding boards, Brenda Buja, Cynthia Gillette-Fox, and Marcia Halliday. We greatly appreciate our resident mathematician/physicist, Dick "Obstacle Illusion" Daniels, Ph.D., and our talented videographer, Heather Daniels.

Marcia Schlehr, using her extensive knowledge of canine structure and locomotion, created the excellent illustrations from just a telephone description. Debbie Spence, Janet Lewis, and Linda Cole gave of their valuable time on short notice to proof the manuscript. Kevin Maughan shared his expertise by imaging the photographs. Our greatest thanks goes to Penny Winegartner, who initially volunteered to "do a little graphic design" for the book and ended up putting her creative stamp on every page.

Last, the authors want to congratulate themselves and each other for knowing when to keep arguing and when to shut up. To co-author a book in new territory is tough and exciting, but to forge a deeper respect and friendship through the process is a real accomplishment.

Table of Contents

Photo by Deborah Lee Miller-Riley

About the Authors

A dog-lover all of her life, Chris Zink got her first dog, an Irish Wolf-hound, the day she graduated from the Ontario Veterinary College with her D.V.M. From an initial interest in obedience mainly as a survival tactic, she gradually became fascinated with all aspects of canine performance. She currently shares her home with three Golden Retrievers and has obtained over 40 titles in obedience, agility, retrieving, and conformation on dogs of several different breeds from three groups.

While competing in canine performance events throughout Canada and the United States, she recognized a significant information gap: owners and trainers wanted to know more about how canine structure affects performance, how medical and physical conditions affect a dog's performance, and how to keep their competition dogs healthy and injury-free. Yet little information was available. She therefore wrote *Peak Performance: Coaching the Canine Athlete*, a comprehensive guide to the dog as an athlete.

Chris presents *Coaching the Canine Athlete* seminars worldwide and regularly writes articles for dog magazines. She is also a consultant on canine sports medicine, evaluating canine structure and locomotion, providing advice on post-injury rehabilitation, and designing individualized conditioning programs for active dogs.

In her other life, Chris is a veterinary pathologist and an Associate Professor at John Hopkins University School of Medicine with over 60 scientific publications. She teaches pathology to medical and veterinary students and does AIDS research.

Julie Daniels is an international agility expert and behaviorist with over 20 years as a dog pro. She started showing dogs in the early 1970's, winning in both the breed and obedience rings. Agility has been Julie's focus since 1987, and she has won many regional championships and national placements with unusual dogs. Her training approach is a win-win philosophy that has turned on the light for many thousands of dogs and their people at her seminars and camps.

Julie has also won awards for her writing, including her best-selling book *Enjoying Dog Agility: From Backyard to Competition*, now in its third printing. A graduate of the University of New Hampshire and a perennial part-time student, her academic background is strong in psychology, writing, and animal science. She studies both teaching and learning and is a dynamic instructor who helps her students examine the training relationship as they work. Through her White Mountain Agility School, Julie has developed a progressive Agility Instructor Certification Course which is turning out skilled trainers who also have the know-how to reach both the human and the canine psyche.

The Daniels family includes three humans, three dogs, a cat, and a horse. Home is a 150-acre tree farm in New Hampshire's White Mountains, where they enjoy a wild and domestic life. Their favorite extracurricular dog sport is hiking in the mountains.

Introduction

Jumping can be so much fun for dogs! Dogs are terrific athletes, and jumping comes naturally to most of them. Like many other creatures, dogs jump not just to clear obstacles, but as an expression of their overall sense of well-being. It is one way that they express confidence and a feeling of strength and vigor. Because it is so natural for a dog to jump over or onto things (like logs in the woods or the couch in the living room), those of us who compete in canine sports such as obedience, agility, and flyball sometimes take jumping for granted. As a result, we may not commit as much time and forethought as we should to training our dogs to jump efficiently and safely. This is especially true of dogs that are considered to be natural jumpers, because early on they display an athletic self-confidence when jumping.

The ability to jump is essential for many different dog sports. With performance standards always rising, many competitors want to know more about the mechanics of canine jumping, about how structure affects a dog's ability to jump, and about why some dogs develop jumping problems.

Dogs are incredibly athletic beings. The ability of most dogs to overcome the effects of gravity and soar over obstacles surpasses that of any horse or human. In addition, dogs are wonderfully adaptable. A properly trained dog can turn abruptly before or after a jump, he can lengthen and shorten his stride on the run to handle unevenly spaced jump sequences or jumps that are set at odd angles, and he can clear jumps of various heights, shapes, and widths.

Nevertheless, a lifetime of jumping in both training and competition can take its toll on a dog. An obedience dog competing in both Open and Utility obedience classes in a single day will jump a total of 5 times. During a typical day of agility competition, a dog will jump at least 7 times if doing AKC^ or UKC^ agility and many times that number if competing at USDAA^ NADAC^, or AAC^ events, which offer games classes in addition to the standard titling classes. A dog competing in a flyball tournament typically jumps 16 jumps (two heats), and many more if his team remains undefeated and he thereby advances in the competition.

During a competition dog's career, repeated jumping definitely increases the stress on the dog's musculoskeletal system — stress that doesn't happen to a dog that lives his life as a couch potato. In addition, performance dogs are at increased risk for injuries as a result of jumping. Many dogs have had their athletic careers abruptly curtailed by serious bony or soft tissue^ injuries. Many more dogs are retired early due to the cumulative stress of repeated minor injuries that add up insidiously, the way that carpal tunnel syndrome sneaks up on humans. It suddenly becomes evident that the dog has a chronic problem that might have been prevented by better maintenance early on.

Given the importance of jumping to canine performance events, it is essential that owners, trainers, and handlers know as much as possible about jumping. Therefore, we undertook a study of canine jumping in an effort to answer the following questions: What are the mechanics of canine jumping? Is there one optimal jumping style? Do dogs of different shapes and sizes need to jump differently? What can be done to reduce the stress on the dog's body during jumping and to prevent injuries due to jumping? What specific techniques should be used to train and condition dogs for the jumping required in obedience, agility, and flyball competition? What can be done to help dogs with jumping problems?

This book contains the answers to these questions as we currently understand them. We continue to be amazed at the athleticism of dogs and at their ability to accommodate to the many challenging variables in the world of performance jumping. We encourage the reader to study videos and still photographs of dogs jumping and compare them with what is presented here. Understanding jumping is a continuous process — there is so much our dogs are trying to teach us!

----

^ Denotes terms that appear in the Glossary.

1. The ABC's of Canine Structure

What an exciting time for dog sports! A smorgasbord of performance activities is available to those who enjoy spending time with their dogs. Obedience, agility, herding tests, lure coursing trials, hunting tests, tracking tests, terrier trials, water rescue, flyball, sledding, draft dog tests, free-style heeling, weight-pulling competitions, Schutzhund trials, and many more events are available for dog owners who want to excel at competition, to obtain titles for their dogs, or who just like to play. While these events provide an abundance of opportunities for us to spend time with our dogs and to experience the thrill of teamwork between human and canine, they have also made us more aware of the need to understand and care for our dogs as athletes.

There is a large body of literature on the care and training of human athletes. Likewise, horse owners, trainers, and veterinarians have studied the equine athlete for centuries. But only now are we beginning to understand in detail the unique nature of canine structure and locomotion and to learn the strengths and weaknesses of dogs as athletes. With this knowledge, the owner/trainer can design appropriate training programs for the canine sport(s) of his choice. Like their human and equine counterparts, dogs in peak condition will perform better, will be less likely to suffer sports injuries, and will remain active and healthy well into their senior years — definitely a win-win situation!

This book concentrates on jumping because it is a movement basic to agility, obedience, and flyball, and is a component of the motions that dogs use in most other canine sports. Jumping at its best is merely an uplifting extension of the canter — a smooth elevation of a gait that comes naturally to the dog. Experienced jumpers are able to make a variety of adjustments to their gait and can select the optimal trajectory for each jump. Such dogs are more confident moving fast on unfamiliar ground because they understand where their bodies are in space and know that they will be able to meet the challenge of most obstacles they will encounter. As a result, all dogs, no matter what their performance aspirations, will benefit from jump training.

Dogs Are Not Horses

The sport of dogs is indebted to the many people that have studied equine structure and locomotion, particularly how horses jump: they have laid much of the groundwork for our understanding of canine locomotion. They have also stimulated those in the dog fancy to examine the athletic nature of the dog in more detail.

Nonetheless, dogs are not horses, and the major differences between the two species should be recognized by those of us that train dogs. We have the opportunity to develop conditioning and training exercises that are appropriate to the dog's superior athletic abilities.

How do we know that the dog is a superior athlete to the horse? One easy way is to compare the jumping ability of these two species. Many dogs can readily jump obstacles twice their height at the withers. In contrast, no horse has yet jumped 1½ times its height.

Compare the structures of the dog and horse, and several differences are immediately apparent. For starters, the dog has more limb angulation than the horse. The effect of this increased angulation is that the dog has a greater stride length relative to its body size than the horse. The dog also has more muscular legs than the horse, whose lower legs are made up mostly of ligaments. These structural advantages provide the dog with greater running speed for its size — about 0.62 mph/lb. for the dog versus 0.04 mph/lb. for the horse. The dog runs 15 times faster!

Another feature of the canine leg that improves the dog's athletic ability is the presence of a separate radius and ulna, the two bones that lie between the carpus (wrist) and the elbow (Fig. 1-1). Because these two bones are separate and lie parallel to each other, the front leg is able to rotate along its axis (making the same motion that we use to turn a screwdriver). This aids

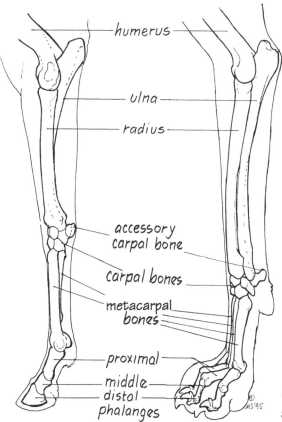

humerus

ulna

radius

accessory
carpal bone

carpal bones

metacarpal
bones

proximal
middle
distal
phalanges

MS'95

Figure 1-1. Side view of bones of the front legs of the horse (left) and dog (right.) In the dog, the radius and ulna are separate, allowing for rotation of the front leg on its axis.

the dog in making fast turns, because the front legs can twist in the direction of the turn. In contrast, the horse's ulna runs only half of the length of the radius, and the two bones are fused. Thus, the horse cannot rotate its front legs to any significant degree, making sharp turns more difficult.

Another structural difference between the legs of the dog and the horse is the conformation of the feet (Fig. 1-2). Whereas the horse's hoof is a single digit with minimal flexibility and sensation, the dog's foot has 4 (or 5) toes that can grip and have a much greater ability to sense and adapt to the terrain. The feet add considerably to the dog's athleticism.

Another structural difference that gives dogs the advantage in jumping is the incredible flexibility of the canine spine. Unlike horses, a dog can arch its spine so that the top of the ribcage rises higher than the withers or the croup (Fig. 1-3). This increased spinal flexibility provides a spring-like action that assists the dog's propulsion. The horse does not have nearly the same spinal flexibility, and this greatly affects its mobility and fluidity over jumps. Dogs are also superior to horses in their ability to flex the spine from side to side, providing them with the ability to make quick turns.

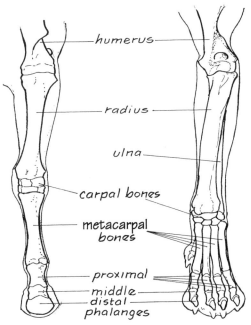

humerus

radius

ulna

carpal bones

metacarpal
bones

proximal
middle
distal
phalanges

Figure 1-2. The horse's foot (left) has just one digit, whereas the dog's foot (right) has four or five. This gives the dog greater ability to grip and adapt to different kinds of footing.

Because of their reduced spinal flexibility, horses are not capable of the wide array of take-off spots, quick turns, and nimble adjustments in stride that our canine athletes can master.

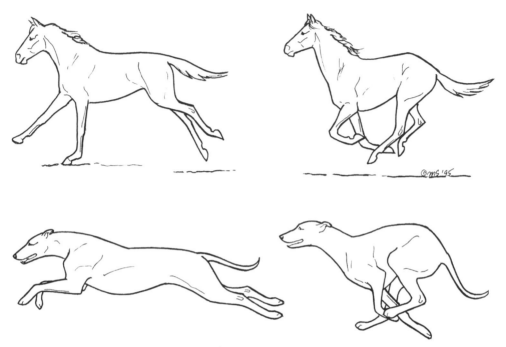

Figure 1-3. The dog has much greater spinal flexibility than the horse.

Evaluating Canine Structure

Body Type

Understanding the dog as an athlete is made somewhat difficult by the tremendous amount of variation among the many dog breeds. During the past several centuries, man has taken advantage of the dog's plastic genetic make-up^, short gestation period, and large litter size to mold his best friend into a variety of shapes and sizes. It is astounding that the Irish Wolfhound and the Dachshund are not only members of the same species, but that both are members of the Hound group.

It is not hard to evaluate canine structure if you remember one main tenet: every part of the canine body that contributes to locomotion is there for a reason. This relationship is often expressed by the maxim "form follows function." Each bump on every bone is there because it has a muscle or ligament attached to it or because it has to absorb the dog's weight while standing or moving. For example, the pads on the backs of a dog's front legs (accessory carpal pads) may look like they are not being used, but they are used during running and jumping, every time the dog bears all of its weight on one front leg.

If you enjoy building or repairing things, then you already understand some of the principles of canine structure. For example, you know that diagonal supports are necessary to stabilize the top, L-shaped corners of a swing set, or the unit will sway from side to side. In the same way, the ABC's of canine structure can be more easily understood by examining the function of each part.

To begin an evaluation of your canine friend, first consider his[1] overall size and body type. Is he light-boned (ectomorphic) like a slim marathon runner? The Afghan Hound and the Italian Greyhound are ectomorphic breeds. Is he heavy-boned (endomorphic) like a heavy-set football player? The Clumber Spaniel and the St. Bernard are endomorphic dogs. The majority of dogs (and humans) are more moderately built (mesomorphic). Mesomorphic breeds include all of the Retrievers, the Border Terrier, the Dalmatian, and the many breeds of dogs that are of medium build with moderate bone.

In addition to these main body types, man has selectively bred dogs to be larger (gigantism) or smaller (dwarfism), and these modifications may help or hinder jumping ability. Within the giant breeds, dogs may be ectomorphic, such as the Borzoi, mesomorphic, such as the Great Dane, or endomorphic, such as the St. Bernard. Breeds that have been bred for small size fall into two categories, both of which have their human counterparts. Those, such as Basset Hounds, Corgis, and Dachshunds, that have the head and body of a larger dog but have shortened legs are termed achondroplastic dwarfs. Those such as Toy Poodles and Papillons with heads, bodies, and legs in proportion to each other are called pituitary dwarfs. Giant breeds and achondroplastic dwarfs are at a disadvantage in jumping, while pituitary dwarfs have a distinct advantage.

One of the easiest ways to objectively evaluate a dog's suitability for performance events is to determine his body weight-to-height ratio. The heavier a dog is in relation to his height, the more effort will be required during locomotion, and the more stress there will be on the musculoskeletal system. Thus, although a Clumber Spaniel and an Afghan Hound may weigh the same, the Clumber Spaniel carries that weight on a shorter frame and will therefore have to exert more effort to move and especially to jump, an exercise that involves resisting the effects of gravity to become airborne and then succumbing to the effects of gravity while landing. Table 1-1 gives sample

----

[1]Throughout this book, for the sake of simplicity, dogs are referred to using the masculine form.

weight:height ratios for a number of individual dogs of a variety of breeds. Weight:height data for the horse and cat are given for comparison.

Table 1-1. Sample weight:height ratios for individuals of a variety of breeds.

Breed	Weight (lb.)	Height (in.)	Weight:Height Ratio
American Staffordshire Terrier	52	18	2.9
Australian Shepherd	42	20	2.1
Basset Hound	45	11	4.1
Bernese Mountain Dog	96	25	3.8
Border Collie	37	20	1.9
Bouvier des Flandres	110	25	4.4
Bullmastiff	135	26	5.2
Doberman Pinscher	78	26	3.0
English Bulldog	50	16	3.1
German Shepherd	74	25	3.0
Golden Retriever	74	24	3.1
Great Dane	150	31	4.8
Great Pyrenees	130	28	4.6
Irish Wolfhound	144	33	4.4
Italian Greyhound	12	15	0.8
Labrador Retriever	64	23	2.8
Mastiff	180	31	5.8
Miniature Dachshund	12	8	1.5
Papillon	7	11	0.6
Pembroke Welsh Corgi	30	12	2.5
Shetland Sheepdog	22	15	1.5
Wheaten Terrier	30	18	1.7
Thoroughbred Horse	1000	64	15.6
Domestic Cat	10	9	1.1

Upon comparing the weight:height ratios for different breeds, it is readily apparent that the lower the weight:height ratio, the easier it is for the dog to jump. We know this intuitively, of course, because we commonly see Papillons jumping three or more times their height to get Mom's attention, whereas it's hard to imagine an English Bulldog pulling that kind of stunt. If these dogs' weights are graphed as a function of their heights, it becomes evident that weight increases at a faster rate than height. The relationship between weight and height is represented by the solid line in Figure 1-4. Thus, the old adage, "the bigger they are, the harder they fall" is true in a literal sense.

In all canine sports, however, jump heights are measured only as a function of height, using a straight line relationship. The slope of the dashed line in Fig.1-4 represents the rate at which AKC jump heights increase with increasing height of the dog. Most breeds are required to jump 1¼ times their height at the withers, regardless of whether the dog is large or small (with some exceptions made for the achondroplastic and giant breeds). The exponential increase in body weight means that the larger dogs are at a disadvantage. They have to exert more effort when jumping and suffer increased stress on the front end when landing than do dogs in the mid-range of sizes. On the other hand, the small dogs have an advantage — it is easier for them to jump the prescribed heights, and there is proportionately less stress on landing. Achondroplastic and endomorphic breeds lie to the left of the solid line because they have greater weight at a given height. Ectomorphic breeds lie to the right of the line because of their lower weight at a given height. One take-home message is obvious: reducing your dog's weight by just a few excess pounds can make an incredible difference in his performance longevity (see Chapter 5 for further discussion of weight).

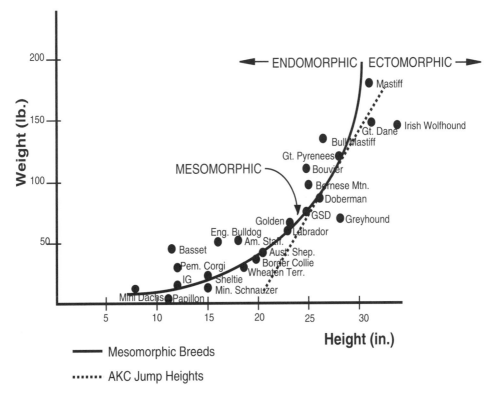

Figure 1-4. Weight:height ratios of dogs of a variety of sizes and shapes. AKC obedience jump heights are determined on the basis of height at the shoulders using a straight line relationship (dashed line).

Although current regulation jump heights in all dog sports are obtained by measuring the dog's height at the withers, the weight:height ratio provides a much better index of the difficulty of jumping. For example, a Basset Hound may be the same height at the withers as a Papillon, but a Basset can only stand and watch in amazement as a Papillon readily jumps an obstacle twice its height! In some sports, such as AKC obedience, breeds such as the

Basset Hound are permitted a jumping handicap, while in other sports such as agility, heavy-set breeds are often at a significant disadvantage. It is important to recognize these differences in weight:height ratio for two reasons. First, you may wish to consider weight:height ratio when getting a new breed. Second, knowing your own dog's weight:height ratio can help you to develop an appropriate conditioning program for him and will give you a new perspective on the effort he expends as your teammate.

It is our observation that dogs with a weight:height ratio of over 4 are in the danger zone for jumping. They should be trained with great care and jumped at full height only when the footing is excellent and the landing soft. Those with a weight:height ratio of 2.5 to 4 are not stressing their musculo-skeletal system as much but are less likely to have a long jumping career than those with a weight:height ratio of less than 2.5.

In addition to weight:height ratio, the length of a dog's legs is another factor in jumping. The greater the length of leg from the ground to the elbow as a percentage of the dog's height at the withers, the greater the advantage to the dog in jumping. The simple reason is that a dog that is longer from the ground to the elbow has a higher center of gravity in relation to its jump height. In addition, during jumping, the majority of the lengthening of the leg takes place above the elbows (Fig. 1-5). Thus, the elbows act as a fulcrum from which the leg extends. It is an advantage in jumping to have that point as high as possible in relation to the height of the jump (which, in turn, is a function of height at the withers). This is like watching two pole vaulters approaching an 18' jump. One has a 14' pole and the other has a 19' pole. Which is more likely to clear the jump?

Another structural factor in jumping is body length as a function of height. Dogs that are significantly longer than they are tall (achondroplastic breeds) bear proportionally more weight on their front legs. They therefore need a stronger front end to lift their heavier fronts, and additional horizontal propulsion in order to clear the jump. In addition to body weight, body length

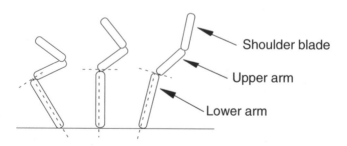

Figure 1-5. When jumping, most of the elongation of the front leg takes place above the elbow.

and leg length also affect jumping ability. Although dogs with certain body types will be handicapped in some performance events, extra conditioning, lowering the dog's weight:height ratio, and sensible training that strengthens rather than strains can make all the difference.

The Front Assembly

The front assembly consists of the scapula (shoulder blade), the humerus (upper arm), the radius and ulna (lower arm), the metacarpals (pastern), and the toes (Fig. 1-6). It is referred to as an assembly because the parts work together and are interdependent. In most breeds, the front end bears approximately 65% of the dog's body weight, and in achondroplastic breeds such as the Basset Hound, it bears considerably more. At the canter and gallop, the front end bears all of the dog's weight for a portion of each stride. When running on flat terrain, the front legs contribute significantly to the dog's horizontal propulsion. When jumping, strong front legs are critical because they lift the dog's front end off the ground at the beginning of the jumping sequence. If the front legs are not strong enough to provide this lift, there is no way that the rear can compensate enough to permit the dog to clear the jump. More important, the front legs also bear the brunt of the concussion upon landing from the jump and help the dog to shift back into a canter upon landing. Because of these functions, a strong, well-structured front assembly is essential for peak performance.

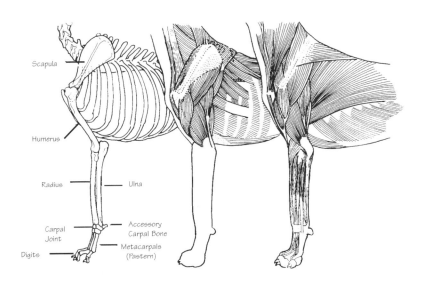

Figure 1-6. Side view of the bones and muscles of the front assembly.

One of the most important things to remember about the structure of the front assembly is that the front legs, unlike the rear legs, are not attached to the dog's body by joints. Instead, they are attached to the ribcage and spine by a series of overlapping muscles that act as a sling upon which the shoulder blades are suspended. This method of attachment greatly increases the range of motion of the front legs. The shoulder blade is able to slide back and forth along the ribcage without the restriction of being directly attached to another bone. However, because muscles and tendons are not as strong as bones and joints, soft-tissue injuries of the shoulders are relatively common in performance dogs, especially in those that do a lot of jumping.

How can you evaluate your dog's front assembly? The two most important components to measure are the shoulder layback and the length of the upper arm. These two features together determine the angulation of the front legs. The term *shoulder layback* refers to how far from vertical the shoulder blades lie. The best way to determine shoulder layback is to stack^ the dog as for the conformation ring. In all breeds, the two front and two back feet (except for the German Shepherd Dog) should be placed side by side pointing straight ahead. When viewing the dog from the side, the lower front leg from the elbow to the carpus should be vertical, as should the rear pastern from the hock to the foot. It is important to stack the dog in this manner because the front legs are very mobile in relation to the body. Depending on how the dog is standing, the shoulder blades may shift towards or away from the vertical, thus making evaluation difficult. Stacking your dog in this manner ensures uniform positioning of both the front and rear legs.

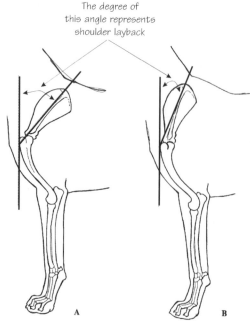

The degree of
this angle represents
shoulder layback

A   B

Figure 1-7. Good shoulder layback (A) vs. upright (B).

Once the dog is stacked, feel one of the scapular bones and find its highest spot adjacent to the spine (Fig. 1-7). Then feel the point at which the scapula meets the upper arm (the point of the shoulder), and draw an imaginary line between these two points. The angle between this line and vertical is a measure of shoulder layback. Generally, the more layback the better. (It is a rare dog indeed that has too much!) It used to be thought that shoulder layback of 45 degrees was ideal, but many now believe that this extreme does not exist and that an angle of 30 degrees is closer to normal.

When the shoulder blade is more vertical (often referred to as upright or straight shoulders), three things happen. First, there is a reduction in the range over which the scapulo-humoral joint (the joint between the shoulder blade and upper arm) can extend. This reduces the amount by which the dog can stretch the front legs forward (reach) and results in a shortened step length (Fig. 1-8). The easiest way to evaluate a dog's reach is to watch the dog from the side as it trots at a moderate speed. Mentally draw a vertical line from the tip of the nose to the ground. As the front leg reaches forward, the foot should intersect that imaginary line close to the ground. Second, upright shoulders reduce the ability of the front legs to absorb the weight of the dog's body as the feet hit the ground, both when gaiting and when jumping. This increases

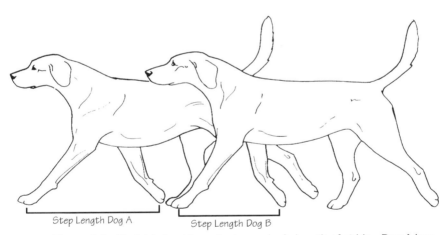

Step Length Dog A

Step Length Dog B

Figure 1-8. Upright shoulders shorten a dog's length of stride. Dog A has proper shoulder layback, whereas Dog B has straight shoulders.

wear and tear on the shoulder and elbow joints, which absorb the majority of the impact during movement. Third, dogs with upright shoulders have less area available for the muscles that extend between the shoulder blade and the upper arm. This can reduce the strength of the forelimbs and thus affect performance.

In addition to shoulder layback, the length of the upper arm also contributes to front limb angulation. As a thumb rule, the upper arm should be approximately the same length as the scapula. To measure these two bones, have someone stack your dog and hold him there. Take a ruler (a 12" ruler will suffice for all but the largest of dogs) and measure the scapula from the

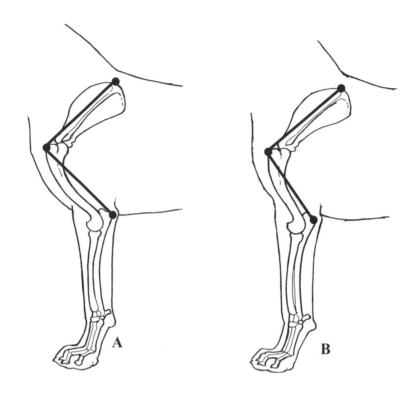

Figure 1-9. A shortened upper arm, as in dog B, draws the lower leg forward. The effect is a reduction in the angulation of the forelimb.

topmost part of the shoulder blade (at the withers) to the point of the shoulder (where the shoulder blade meets the upper arm). To measure the upper arm, just hold the end of the ruler at the point of the shoulder and swing the other end of the ruler down to the point of the elbow (the canine equivalent of the funny bone; Fig. 1-9). Many dogs have a shorter upper arm than shoulder blade. The shorter the upper arm, the closer to vertical the upper arm will be when the dog is standing. The effect is similar to that of an upright shoulder, a reduction in the ability to reach forward, reduced muscle mass between the scapula and the upper arm, and hence a reduction in the length of stride and an increase in concussion. The effects of an upright shoulder and shortened upper arm are additive. Active performance dogs with both problems are much more prone to shoulder injuries and have a greater chance of developing arthritis of the shoulder and/or elbow.

The Rear Assembly

The rear assembly consists of the pelvis, the femur (upper leg), the tibia/fibula (lower leg), the metatarsals (rear pastern), and the toes (Fig. 1-10). The rear legs are attached to the pelvis and spine by the hip joints. The hip joint is a ball-and-socket joint which allows the leg not only to move forward and back, but also to turn outward. Without this joint, it would be much more difficult to give your upside-down dog a tummy rub! The bones and muscles of the rear leg work together in unison. The stifle (knee) joint cannot be completely flexed or extended without also flexing/extending the hock joint. The positions of the muscles and tendons of the rear leg make it impossible to do otherwise. The stifle and hock are thus functionally linked, and when there is an injury to one, the function of the other is often affected.

Angulation is as important in the rear legs as in the front. How can one judge rear angulation? Again, start by placing the dog in a show pose

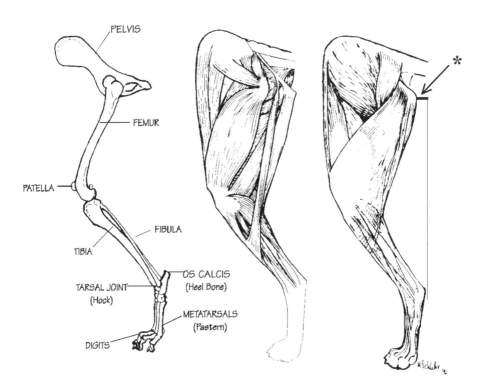

Figure 1-10. The bones and muscles of the rear leg. Dogs with greater rear angulation have a greater distance (asterisk) between the back of the pelvis and an imaginary vertical line drawn up from the rear pastern.

with the rear pasterns vertical from the hock to the feet. Draw an imaginary vertical line (Fig. 1-10) upwards from the rear pastern. If this line meets the bone at the back of the pelvis, the dog has minimal rear angulation. The farther behind the pelvis this imaginary line is, the greater the rear angulation.

How much is enough rear angulation? Unfortunately, there is no simple answer to this question. The greater the angulation, the more potential for propulsion from the rear. Picture a frog without rear angulation and guess how far he can jump! But there is also a trade-off. The more angulated the rear, the less stable it is. Perhaps that is why a frog doesn't stand on its rear legs but instead sits on its behind! The most stable conformation would be a perfectly straight leg. That is why the ancients used columns to hold up their buildings. Of course, it would be of no use to make the legs of a dog as straight (and stable) as a column, because the dog has to move. Thus, there is an inverse relationship between stability and propulsion. Depending on the dog's function (and often to a greater extent on the whim of humans), dogs may have more or less rear angulation. In addition, individuals within each breed may have extremes of angulation.

The most extreme example of rear angulation is seen in the German Shepherd Dog. This extreme rear angulation gives these dogs the propulsion they need to be able to perform their characteristic, flashy gait: the flying trot. When a trotting German Shepherd Dog is viewed from the side, it flies across the ground. When viewed from the rear, however, the hocks often wobble as the weight is borne on each leg. In this breed, stability has been intentionally sacrificed for propulsion. In contrast, a number of breeds, including the Akita, the Chow, the Shar-Pei and others, have minimal rear angulation. In these breeds, stability is preferred over propulsion. As a guard dog, the Akita may need the stability of a straighter rear to stand its ground against strangers. Most dog breeds fall between these two extremes of angulation, enabling them to have a certain measure of both stability and propulsion.

The Spinal Column and Tail

The spinal column is the main support system for the canine body. Like the horizontal bar at the top of a swing set, it is responsible for stabilizing several bodies of weight (the legs) that swing back and forth. And, just as the swing set has diagonal support bars at each of the top corners, the front and rear legs are attached to the spine, not by vertical bones, but by bones (the shoulder blades and pelvis) that meet the spinal cord at an angle. In addition to its stabilizing function, the spinal cord must also be flexible enough to permit a wide variety of movements, including running, jumping, and turning. This is accomplished by dividing the spine into a series of 50 bones, each of which is attached to those on either side by means of a flexible intervertebral disk and two joints - one on each side of the vertebral bone. These attachments allow the bones to move in relation to each other while still remaining attached, much like the cars of a long train.

The vertebrae of the spinal column can be divided into five groups (Fig. 1-11): the cervical (neck) vertebrae, the thoracic (chest) vertebrae, the lumbar (loin) vertebrae, the sacral (pelvic) vertebrae, and the coccygeal (tail) vertebrae. Each of these sections has a different function, although all work together in movement. The seven cervical vertebrae support the head which is lifted and lowered to assist with propulsion, much as a runner pumps his arms. Likewise, the swinging of the head from side to side assists in turning.

A major function of the 15 thoracic vertebrae is to support the attachment of the ribs which enclose the heart and lungs — organs that are critical to locomotion. Because of the attached ribs, this area of the spinal column is the least flexible.

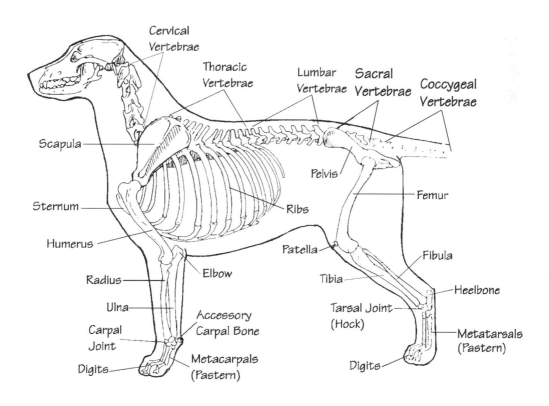

Figure 1-11. The bones of the dog.

The thoracic vertebrae join the seven lumbar vertebrae which are highly flexible. Because of the differences in flexibility between the thoracic and lumbar vertebrae, the point where these two sections meet (the thoraco-lumbar junction) is under a great deal of stress. This is a common area for injury or soreness in the performance dog.

Figure 1-12. This dog is using the weight of his tail to help swing the rear end to the left in preparation for a right turn.

The next section of spine is the sacrum. The three bones of the sacrum are fused and form one larger bone to which the pelvis is attached. The final section of spine is the tail. There are 20 tail bones in dogs that have not had their tails docked. The tail provides balance during movement. It helps the dog to turn on the ground and is important in jumping. It also helps the dog to raise and lower the rear end and assists the dog in turning in mid-air (Fig. 1-12). (At that instant, the tail is indeed wagging the dog!) For this reason, dogs with docked tails are at a disadvantage, particularly when jumping at their maximal height and when rapid changes of direction are required. The shorter the tail, the greater compensation must be made through rear limb movement and spinal flexibility.

The Feet

Dogs' feet are very important in performance. The feet have to be tough enough to be useful on a variety of different terrains, yet soft enough to absorb the impact of the dog's weight, even when landing from a jump. They also must be flexible enough to grip rough ground and to assist the dog in turning. Dogs' feet can be likened to the tires of a car. Both the feet and tires form the point at which the moving object meets the stationary ground: they provide the traction needed for acceleration and turning. It is said that the perfect car tire has not yet been invented. Car racing teams are forever changing tires in the middle of a race and experimenting with new tire formulations. By comparison, the feet of a dog are a much better tool!

The toughness of the canine foot is provided by the thick keratin surface of the pads. Keratin is a waterproof protein that is laid down in multiple overlapping layers. New keratin is continually being produced to replace the layers that are lost at the surface. This is why, unlike car tires, a dog's feet rarely loses its treads. The toes are cushioned by a thick layer of elastic tissue within the pad; this pad compresses under the weight of the dog and then returns to its original shape. The flexibility of the canine foot is a function of the positions of the bones of the toes. Instead of lying flat on the ground, the toes are actually bent in an upside down U, with just the tips of the toes touching the ground, much like the position of a pianist's fingers just before he starts to play. This allows the toes to bend further or to straighten in response to the terrain.

There are two main shapes of feet in purebred dogs: the cat foot and the hare foot. The cat foot is rounded, with each of the toes radiating outward from the center of the foot. The hare foot is elongated, with the toes pointing more frontward. Dogs such as the Afghan Hound that were bred to hunt game on rough or rocky terrain have cat feet. Their feet function like the wide, deep-treaded tires of all-terrain vehicles — they help the dog to grip uneven ground and to turn quickly. Breeds such as Greyhounds that are bred for running over flat terrain tend to have more elongated feet. Their feet are like the tires of Formula One racing cars that have no treads in order to increase friction against the road and thus assist with forward movement.

A discussion of the dog's foot would not be complete without mention of the dew claws. In most dogs, the dew claws are attached to the bones of the pastern by a joint. When dogs canter or gallop there is one moment when a single front leg remains on the ground, bearing the dog's full weight (Fig. 1-13). At that point, even in the lightest dogs, the pastern is flat on the ground and the carpal pad is cushioning the carpal joint as it hits the ground. At that moment, the dew claw is in contact with the ground and can catch the ground as the dog rotates its leg on turning. This allows the dog to take full advantage of the ability of the front leg to rotate on its axis. Some people who compete with sighthounds in lure-coursing have observed an increased incidence of front leg and foot injuries in dogs who have had their dew claws

Figure 1-13. When dogs bear all of their weight on one front leg, the carpus is hyperextended and rests on the ground.

Photo by Victoria Janicki

removed. For this reason, some people prefer not to have their puppies' dew claws removed. They prefer to give their performance dogs the advantage of a functional dew claw and risk possible injury to the dew claw that might necessitate its removal later in life.

This completes our guided tour of the canine athlete's body. A knowledge of canine functional anatomy will improve the way you and your canine friend work together as a team. Knowing what a remarkable athlete the dog is should increase your enthusiasm for canine sports and improve your confidence in your dog's abilities. In addition, a knowledge of canine structure and its relationship to performance will help you to recognize problems soon after they occur, and thus will contribute to your dog's general health and longevity as an athlete.

2. How Do They Do It?

Now that you know what an amazing athlete your canine teammate is, you probably have all kinds of new questions like, "How, exactly, do dogs jump? Does it matter whether their back legs are tucked underneath or held straight out behind? How far from the jump should a dog take off?" The answers to these and many more questions are provided in this chapter on the biomechanics of jumping.

The Mechanics of Jumping

Simply speaking, jumping is just an extension of the canter, in which the dog adds some more vertical lift and horizontal propulsion in order to clear an obstacle. In the canter, the rear legs push off, one slightly ahead of the other, driving the body forward. The front legs then reach out and land one ahead of the other (Fig. 2-1). The front legs pull the dog's body forward as the dog flexes his spine, lifts his rear legs, and swings them forward for the next step.

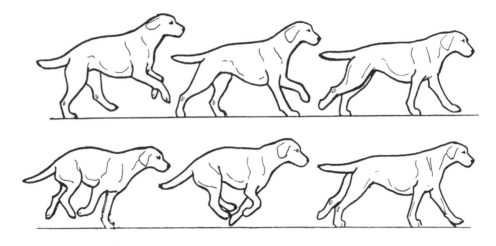

Figure 2-1. The canter. This dog is leading with the left leg.

The front leg that reaches forward and touches down ahead of the other is referred to as the lead leg^. Most dogs have a preferred lead leg but can also shift to use the other front leg as lead if necessary. A dog may change leads when he is tired and wishes to utilize a different set of muscles for a while. A dog may also choose to change leads to make a sharp turn or to allow him to arrive at his preferred take-off spot for a jump. Dogs can be taught to identify when a lead change is required and to change easily from the right to the left lead and back. This results in improved agility, increased speed and smoothness of performance, and in a reduced risk of performance-related injuries.

The canter is a gait that easily allows the dog to alter his speed and stride length. This makes it an ideal gait to use in jumping because it provides the dog with the flexibility to make last-minute changes in speed and stride length so that he will arrive at his preferred take-off spot.

Regardless of breed or size, all dogs jump using the following sequence of movements (Figs. 2-2 & 2-3). As the dog approaches the jump, he places his front feet, one slightly ahead of the other, at a take-off spot on the ground in front of the jump. This point is determined by a number of factors: the speed of the dog, the height of the jump, the weight:height ratio of the dog, the footing, the strength and conditioning of the dog, and the dog's confidence in his ability to clear the jump. As the front legs are planted, the dog lowers his head and flexes the front legs a little. He then flexes his spine and brings the rear legs forward, placing them on the ground slightly ahead of the front feet. The dog then extends the front legs, pushing the front of his

Figure 2-2. The jump is an extention of the canter.

body upwards and raising his head to assist with upward thrust. The rear legs are then extended, propelling the dog's body upward and forward over the jump. Once the dog is in the air, he lowers his head closer to the outstretched front legs in order to help with forward thrust and to reduce drag. At the apex of the arc, the dog should lower his head and lift his tail to help rotate the body forward and down. He stretches the front legs forward and down, one ahead of the other, to prepare for the landing. After the front legs have hit the ground, the rear legs are drawn forward under the dog's body to absorb some of the impact of landing and to continue the canter.

Figure 2-3a

Figure 2-3b

Photos by Anthony Benson

Figure 2-3. The dog is jumping from right to left. In (a) she has raised the front end by extending the front legs. She then straightens the rear legs (b) propelling her body forward over the jump. After clearing the jump (c), she stretches her front legs forward to land, and (d) the rear legs follow to continue the canter.

Figure 2-3c

Figure 2-3d

During the jumping sequence, the dog's body can be viewed as a wheel with its axle resting on a wire (Fig. 2-4). The axle represents the dog's center of mass, and the wire represents the dog's trajectory. Just as the trajectory of a thrown ball does not change after it leaves the hand, so the trajectory of the dog's center of mass does not change after the dog has left the ground. What can change, however, is the positioning of the dog's body around the center of mass. Just as a ball might spin forward or backward, the dog's body rotates forward and back. By kicking his rear legs up and back, for example, the dog effectively spins the wheel a little bit clockwise (when viewed as in Fig. 2-4). By dropping the rear legs, he spins the wheel a little counterclockwise. Thus, by raising or lowering the head or tail or changing the position of the legs, the dog is able to spin himself on his center of mass to assist him in clearing the jump.

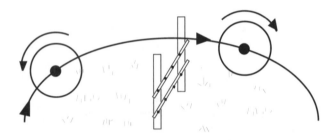

Figure 2-4. As the dog jumps, his body initially rotates counterclockwise on his center of gravity. After he reaches the apex of the trajectory, he rotates clockwise.

In addition to helping the dog clear the jump, these changes in position can affect how he lands. For example, if he raises his head soon after the apex of the trajectory, the center of gravity will be shifted more to the rear. This causes the rear legs to land at the same time or shortly after the front legs. This jumping style is seen in some terriers and other dogs with straight fronts (Fig. 2-5). By landing on all four legs at once, there is less force of impact on the front end. However, the dog pays a price for this jumping style. When landing only on the front legs, the force of the impact travels up the front legs and is dissipated by the flexion of the front legs and the spine. If a dog lands on all four feet at the same time, the force of impact travels up both the front and rear legs, and opposing forces meet in the spinal column, causing increased stress on the bones, muscles, and ligaments. In addition, the front end should land first to allow a smooth continuation of the canter upon landing. A dog dropped squarely on the ground has difficulty moving directly into a canter.

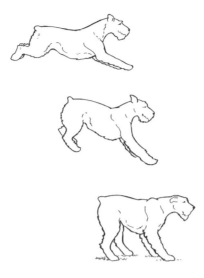

Figure 2-5. Dogs with straighter fronts sometimes land so that the rear legs hit the ground soon after the front legs in order to reduce concussion on the front.

While on the subject, it is worth mentioning an observation we made while viewing hundreds of dogs starting their agility runs. Dogs that are left standing at the start line tend to trot a few steps prior to breaking into a canter in preparation for the first jump. If the start line is situated close to the first jump, this frequently leaves the dog with just one canter stride before taking off to clear the jump. In contrast, dogs that are left in a sit at the start line tend to spring forward with their rear legs and begin moving at a canter immediately. This allows them to accelerate faster and to collect or extend themselves appropriately in preparation for the first jump. It was also evident that the first jump in an agility trial was usually taken with less certainty and often with a different jumping style than the remainder of the jumps in the course. This first-jump phenomenon was evident in the vast majority of dogs and suggests that handlers should make specific plans to help the dog accommodate to that first jump. This may be done by leaving the dog at a sit at the beginning of the course and by placing him well behind the start line. (More on jumping for agility in Chapter 7.)

That's fine for agility, but what about obedience? In obedience, every jump is the first jump. This is one of the issues that makes obedience jumping difficult. Added to that, the solid jumps prevent the dog from seeing conditions on the far side of the jump. This can add a significant measure of uncertainty to the obedience jumps. (See Chapter 6 for more on jumping for obedience.)

The Trajectory

Trajectory is the term for the path through the air that the dog takes while jumping. There has been much discussion of the correct trajectory for jumping, and some confusion has occurred because of attempts to apply the principles of horse jumping to dogs. In Grand Prix horse jumping (in which the jumps are set at the highest heights that horses are capable of jumping), it is desirable for the horse's trajectory to be that of a bascule, an arc shaped like a half-circle (Fig. 2-6). To achieve this trajectory, the horse should leave the ground at a point as far away from the jump as the jump is high. However, the superior athletic abilities of the dog and significant differences between canine sporting events and equine jumping events mean that dogs have a much larger repertoire of jumping styles from which to choose.

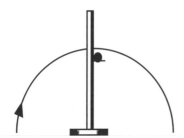

Figure 2-6. The round trajectory of the bascule.

Dogs that jump with a flatter trajectory experience less deceleration and less vertical impact on landing and thus suffer less stress to the front end. Over the lifetime of an active dog, the reduced stress on the carpal joints, elbows, and shoulders means fewer soft tissue^ injuries and a reduced incidence and/or severity of arthritis, a condition that afflicts many performance dogs in their later years. The need to lessen the stress on the ligaments, tendons, and joints of the front end by jumping with a flatter trajectory becomes even more important when dogs are asked to turn after landing as happens repeatedly in agility and obedience. It is therefore important to train dogs to jump with a flatter trajectory when appropriate, and most dogs have the athletic ability to do so.

Factors That Affect Trajectory

- speed
- jump height
- weight:height ratio
- footing
- dog's strength and conditioning
- whether it is necessary to turn after landing
- dog's attitude

What are the factors that contribute to a flatter trajectory? First, the dog must have adequate speed. When the dog leaves the ground to jump, it first must resist the effects of gravity to become airborne and then succumb to the effects of gravity upon landing. Think back to high school physics for a moment. When Isaac Newton held a Chihuahua under one arm and a Rottweiler under the other and dropped them from a balcony, which one hit the ground first? Both dogs accelerated toward the ground at a speed of 32 ft/sec^2 and hit the ground at the same time. (We are assuming air resistance to be negligible.) The time that it takes each dog to fall is independent of the dog's weight. When a dog jumps, vertical deceleration occurs at a rate of 32 ft/sec^2 during the first half of the trajectory, and after the dog reaches the top of its arc, it accelerates toward the ground at 32 ft/sec^2. It takes the same amount of time for the up and down parts of the journey. Therefore, if the dog is to jump with a flatter trajectory and cover more ground in the same amount of time, he must be moving at a greater speed (Fig. 2-7).

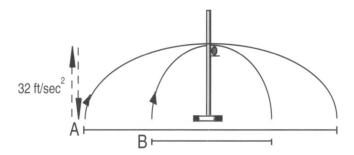

32 ft/sec^2

Figure 2-7. The physics of a flatter trajectory. Vertical acceleration and deceleration take the same amount of time, regardless of the dog's trajectory. Therefore, to cover the greater distance required to achieve a flatter trajectory, Dog A must be moving at a greater speed than Dog B.

There are circumstances in which it is not ideal for a dog to be moving very fast, and at these times it is neither ideal nor possible for the dog to jump with a very flat trajectory. The canine sports that most often preclude dogs from jumping with a flat trajectory are USDAA agility for dogs that jump 30" and AKC obedience for dogs that jump approximately 26" or more. In both of these sports, limitations with respect to the amount of room between jumps, or between the ring barriers and the jumps, reduce the larger dog's choices of jumping style. A rounder trajectory is often the safest one in these circumstances. Using the techniques outlined in this book, dogs can be taught to confidently judge the space available to them and to select the most appropriate jumping trajectory.

Another factor that may alter a dog's trajectory is the height of the jump. The higher the jump, the more effort is required to resist the effects of gravity. This may make it necessary to sacrifice horizontal speed for vertical thrust. The result is a rounder trajectory. This effect is seen when one compares the trajectory of horses competing in Grand Prix jumping events with that of horses in steeplechase events. The jumps in a steeplechase are lower and set farther apart so that the horse is able to achieve the speed necessary to clear the jump with a flatter trajectory. Use of a flatter trajectory is well known among steeplechasers, where some talented jumping horses are known for "making up in the air what they lack on the flat."

The weight:height ratio of the dog also affects the trajectory. The greater the weight:height ratio, the rounder the trajectory, because a greater weight must be moved over a jump of a given height. For example, a Whippet and a Clumber Spaniel may be the same height and thus required to clear a jump of the same height, but because of its greater weight, the Clumber Spaniel will use a rounder trajectory. There are other reasons for a confident jumper to choose a rounder trajectory. A dog may sense that the footing is not optimal and may use a rounded trajectory to avoid slipping on take-off or landing. Dogs that are not very strong or lack condition will usually select a rounder trajectory. If a turn is required immediately after landing, the experienced jumper will select a rounder trajectory so that he is in position to make the turn (Fig. 2-8). Dogs that are not feeling well or are not particularly motivated to jump will use a rounder trajectory because they do not achieve

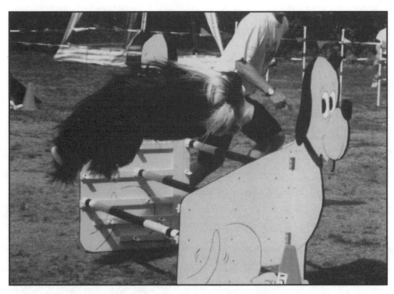

Figure 2-8. This Bearded Collie is jumping with a rounded trajectory because he knows that he will have to turn on landing.

Figure 2-9. This Cairn Terrier is using a flat trajectory because the footing is excellent, the jump is low, and life is good!

the speed necessary for a flatter trajectory. Nonetheless, a dog that has been properly conditioned and correctly trained to jump, *all other things being equal*, will select the flattest (and hence safest) trajectory (Fig. 2-9).

Jumping Styles

Jumping style represents a combination of the positions of the rear legs, front legs, and head at the apex of the jump trajectory. The combined positions of all of these body parts determine whether the spinal column is rounded, flat and stretched out, or arched. Although most dogs have a favorite jumping style, experienced jumpers mix and match these positions and select among them, or even change them in mid-air, depending on the circumstances.

Rear Leg Position
Is it better for a dog to jump with his legs tucked underneath his body or stretched out behind? What about dangling? These are questions that many exhibitors ask. The answer is that there is no one correct jumping style for all dogs and all circumstances. Confident, experienced jumpers have a repertoire of several jumping styles that they draw from, depending on the situation.

There are five major rear leg positions that dogs may adopt in jumping (Table 2-1). In the **full stretch** (Fig. 2-10), the dog's rear legs are fully extended and stretched straight out behind him, parallel to the ground. In order to assume this position, a dog must have excellent spinal flexibility, and for this reason, short-backed, broad-chested dogs tend to use this position less often than longer, slimmer dogs. The full stretch is most often adopted when the dog is jumping with good speed and a flat trajectory. This is a business-like position adopted by dogs that are jumping with intensity.

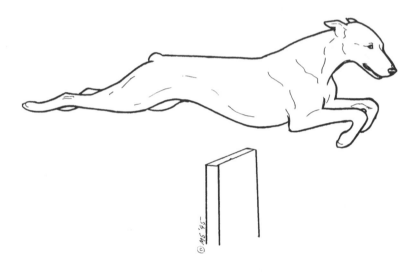

Photo by Mary Jo Sminkey

Figure 2-10. In the full stretch, the rear legs are fully extended behind the dog.

The **relaxed stretch** is similar to the full stretch, but instead of being fully extended, the dog's legs are somewhat relaxed while still held out behind the body (Fig. 2-11). Dogs that adopt this position are usually confident about the jumping conditions, but are not feeling as intense about jumping as those utilizing a full stretch.

Photo by Mary Jo Sminkey

Figure 2-11. The relaxed stretch is similar to the full stretch, but the rear legs are more relaxed.

The **full tuck** is a position in which the dog's legs are completely flexed and held tight underneath the body, with the rear pasterns parallel to the ground (Fig. 2-12). Dogs generally utilize the full tuck when they are jumping carefully. The full tuck position allows them to keep their rear legs ready to reach towards the ground. Dogs use the full tuck position when they are jumping a height that is maximal for their size or jumping ability, or when they are required to turn soon after jumping. Some dogs prefer to use this position for the majority of jumps.

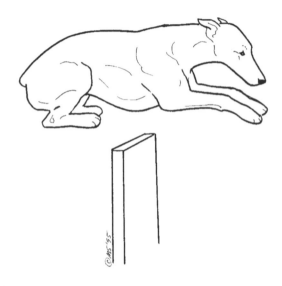

Figure 2-12. In the full tuck, the rear legs are completely flexed and held tight underneath the body, with the rear pasterns parallel to the ground.

In the **back tuck**, the rear legs are flexed and held tight against the body, but instead of being held under the body, the legs are tilted backwards and held against the dog's butt, with the rear pasterns positioned almost perpendicular to the ground (Fig. 2-13). This position is generally used by strong jumpers that are intense about jumping and have flexible spines. It is frequently used by dogs that have to turn immediately upon landing. The backward tilt of the rear legs allows the dog to readily swivel the pelvis to one side so that the legs will land on the ground in a position to push off for the next jump (see In-air Modifications).

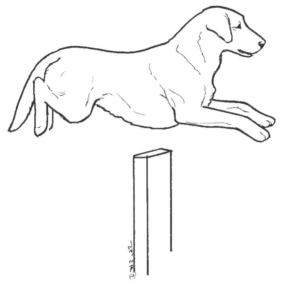

Photo by Jutta Hammermueller

Figure 2-13. In the back tuck, the rear legs are flexed and held tightly to the body, but instead of being held underneath the body, the legs are tilted backwards and held against the dog's butt, with the rear pasterns positioned almost perpendicular to the ground.

The **relaxed tuck** is a position in which the upper part of the dog's legs are flexed, but the legs from the hock to the pastern are relaxed and hanging down, perpendicular to the ground (Fig. 2-14). This jumping position is typical of certain breeds, especially the Labrador Retriever, but all dogs may choose this jumping style when they feel confident about the jump, yet want the rear legs to be somewhat ready for action.

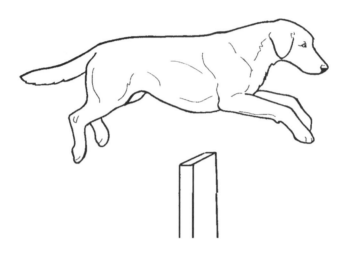

Figure 2-14. In the relaxed tuck, the upper part of the dog's rear legs are flexed, but the legs from the hock to the pastern are relaxed and hanging down, perpendicular to the ground.

Table 2-1 Jumping Positions

Body Part	Position	Explanation
Rear Legs	full stretch	Rear legs fully extended and stretched straight out behind dog, horizontal to the ground.
	relaxed stretch	Similar to full stretch, but with the rear legs more relaxed while still held out behind.
	full tuck	Rear legs are completely flexed and held tight under the body with rear pasterns parallel to the ground.
	back tuck	Rear legs are tightly flexed and held close to body, but tilted backward with the rear pasterns almost perpendicular to the ground.
	relaxed tuck	Rear legs are loosely flexed, with the lower leg from the hocks to the toes hanging.
Front Legs	stretch	Front legs reach out in front of the dog, either stretched out or relaxed.
	tuck	Front legs are held under the chest, often folded at the carpus.
Head	up	Head is held up, away from the legs.
	down	Head is held low and forward.

Front Leg Position

Because the head and front legs almost always clear the jump, their positions are not nearly as important to the outcome of the jump as the position of the rear legs. A certain front leg position is not necessarily associated with a specific rear leg position or head position. Dogs have a wide range of front leg positions, from stretched to tucked. In the **stretch**, the dog's front legs are extended out in front (Fig. 2-13), with the paws ahead of the nose (except in dogs with really short legs). Note that this is the position at the apex of the trajectory. After the apex of the trajectory, all dogs stretch their front legs out in preparation for landing. In the **tuck**, the dog's legs are flexed at the shoulder and elbow so that the legs lie under the neck and chest. Some dogs keep their carpi (wrists) straight, and others flex the carpi (Fig. 2-10). Perhaps because they generally do not cause a problem with clearing the jumps, there doesn't seem to be a clear advantage to adopting one front leg position over another, although dogs often choose one front leg position and stick with it.

Head Position

There are two main head positions: **head up** and **head down**. Dogs that are confident in their ability to clear a jump often use the head up position (Fig. 2-15), while jumps that require more concentrated effort may call for the head-down approach (Fig. 2-16). The head-up position can be problematic because the dog needs to raise its head just before the front legs hit the ground on landing to reduce the stress on the front end. If a dog already has his head held very high, he will not be able to use it in this way.

In-Air Modifications

Sometimes a dog may misjudge the physical requirements necessary to clear an obstacle or may change his mind in mid-air about how he wants to handle a jump. For example, he may misjudge the take-off spot or slip as he pushes off from the ground and thus may not have adequate propulsion to clear the jump. Or he may take off using a certain jumping style and at some point obtain new information (such as a handler belatedly telling him that the next jump requires a sharp left turn upon landing) that requires a change in his jumping style. To cope with these situations, confident jumpers have a number of in-air modifications ready to apply to their jumping style when necessary for safety or to make their movements more efficient.

Photo by Herb Bradt

Figure 2-15. This Doberman is jumping with a cocky head-up style.

Photo by Chris Peach

Figure 2-16. This Doberman is jumping with an intense, head-down style.

The **kick-back** is usually performed by larger dogs, when jumping with their rear legs in a tuck. Just after the apex of the trajectory, the dog straightens his rear legs, kicking them up and back (Fig. 2-17). This raises the rear end and prevents the rear legs from hitting the jump. Sometimes a dog will also spread the rear legs apart to reduce the chance of them hitting the jump (Fig. 2-18). Some dogs use these modifications as a matter of routine, while others use them only when necessary to clear a jump.

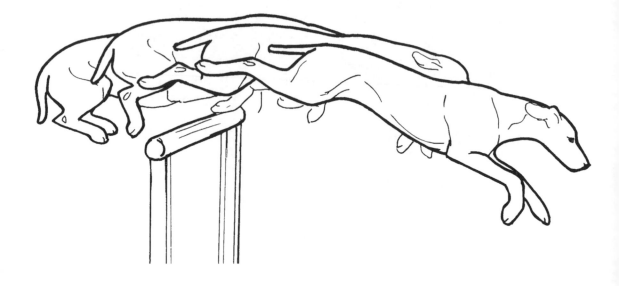

Figure 2-17. The kick-back is used to help the rear legs clear the jump.

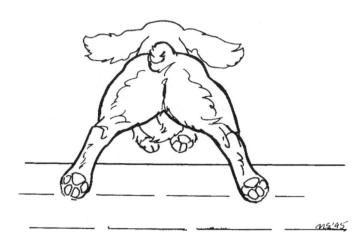

Figure 2-18. Some dogs spread their rear legs apart to help them clear the jump.

The **kick-forward**, on the other hand, is used almost exclusively by small dogs, frequently those of the achondroplastic breeds. At some point before the apex of the trajectory, the dog realizes that he doesn't have enough speed or horizontal thrust to clear the jump unless some extra effort is applied. At that point, he swings his rear legs forward so that they lie under the belly, pointing straight ahead (Fig. 2-19). This gives the dog a little extra forward thrust and, at the same time, gets the rear legs out of the way of the jump.

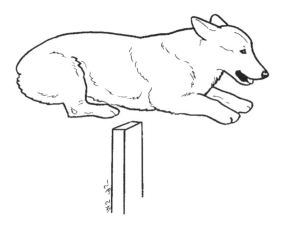

Figure 2-19. The kick-forward may be used to provide a little extra forward thrust and, at the same time, get the rear legs out of the way of the jump.

The **hip-swivel** is one of the best examples of the dog's incredible adaptability in jumping. The swivel is used when a dog plans to turn sharply after landing from a jump. In order to execute a hip-swivel, the dog must be in a tucked position—usually a back tuck. If the dog has started the jump in a stretched position, he will change to a back-tuck position prior to the hip-swivel. Essentially, the hip-swivel involves rotating the pelvis (and hence, the rear legs) to one side or the other along the long axis of the spine. If a dog is going to turn right upon landing, the pelvis rotates clockwise (when viewed from behind; Fig. 2-20). Then, when the dog lands, the rear legs will already be pointing in a direction that will provide thrust to the right. The dog also uses the weight and strength of his head and tail to assist in the process of turning. The hip-swivel is used by confident jumpers to execute turns more quickly and safely.

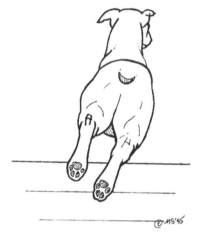

Figure 2-20. The hip swivel is used to prepare for a turn after landing.

On-Ground Adjustments

With proper training and enough experience, a dog learns to judge the distance between jumps and is already assessing these distances well ahead of the jump he is currently executing. He then makes modifications to his stride length between jumps so that he will be at the appropriate take-off spot for each jump. The canter is an ideal gait to use for jumping, because at a canter, the dog's stride length (the distance between the points at which the lead leg hits the ground on two successive strides) can readily be altered. Stride length is partly a function of speed. A dog that is traveling faster will have a longer stride length because it is putting more power into limb and spinal extension, thus driving the dog further across the ground. Stride length is also a function of the length and flexibility of the dog's back, the length of his legs, and the degree of angulation of his front and rear legs.

Angulation is a particularly important factor. Two dogs may be of the same height and have the same length backs, but the one with greater front and rear angulation will be able to take longer strides. This is why it is not possible to accurately determine a dog's stride length by measuring the dog's height, leg length, or body length. Further, most dogs are comfortable cantering within a range of stride lengths. This gives them the ability to adapt to a variety of different jumping sequences.

Two of the on-ground adjustments that dogs make when approaching a jump are **extensions** and **collections**. When extending his stride, the dog increases the stride length by extending the rear legs completely to increase

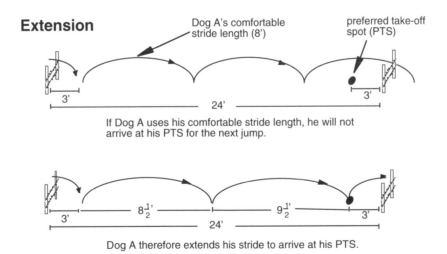

Extension

Dog A's comfortable stride length (8')

preferred take-off spot (PTS)

3'   24'   3'

If Dog A uses his comfortable stride length, he will not arrive at his PTS for the next jump.

3' $8\frac{1}{2}$' $9\frac{1}{2}$'   3'

24'

Dog A therefore extends his stride to arrive at his PTS.

Figure 2-21. Dog A is extending his stride to arrive at his prefered take-off spot.

the horizontal propulsion, stretching the spine out and reaching forward as far as possible with the front legs to increase the amount of ground covered with each stride. When collecting himself, the dog shortens his stride length by reducing the extension of the spine and legs and transferring some of his horizontal momentum to vertical movement.

For example, in Figure 2-21, there are two jumps 24 feet apart. Judging by his weight:height ratio and current level of fitness, Dog A would prefer to take off and land 3 feet from the jump. This leaves 18 feet between the jumps for striding. Dog A's size, angulation, and current speed dictate that a comfortable stride length is 8 feet, and being a well-trained, confident jumper, he recognizes that, if he takes two 8-foot strides, he will end up 5 feet from the second jump — too far for him to take off and clear the jumps safely. He therefore decides to adjust his stride length on the fly, extending it to two strides of 9 feet each (or more likely an initial stride of 8½ feet and a second of 9½ feet). In this way, he will arrive at his preferred take-off spot for the second jump.

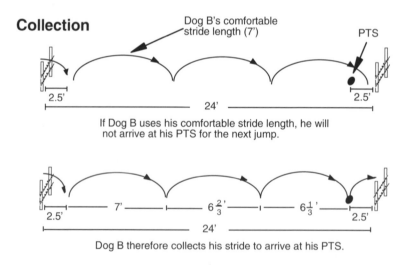

Collection

Dog B's comfortable stride length (7')

PTS

2.5'   24'   2.5'

If Dog B uses his comfortable stride length, he will not arrive at his PTS for the next jump.

2.5'   7' $6\frac{2}{3}$' $6\frac{1}{3}$'   2.5'

24'

Dog B therefore collects his stride to arrive at his PTS.

Figure 2-22. Dog B is collecting his stride to arrive at his preferred take-off spot.

Using the same jump setup (Fig. 2-22), Dog B, who has a greater weight:height ratio than Dog A, prefers to take off and land 2½ feet from the jump. This results in a span of 19 feet to stride between the jumps. His structure and speed dictate that a stride length of 7 feet would be comfortable, but if he takes two 7-foot strides, he will be too far from the second jump to attempt it, and if he takes three 7-foot strides, he will be too close to the jump to clear it safely. Therefore, he collects himself — shortens his stride to 6⅔ feet (or, more likely, takes three strides of 7 feet, 6⅔ feet, and 6⅓ feet, thus providing a more gradual change in speed) so that three strides will place him at the appropriate take-off spot for the second jump. These illustrations should also serve to emphasize the importance of giving commands in agility well before the dog arrives at the obstacle — the dog needs time to plan ahead!

Another on-ground adjustment involves **changing leads.** As you recall, the lead leg is the front leg that lands ahead of the other in the canter. The lead leg is often the dog's stronger or more dominant leg, because that leg has to be strong and flexible enough to reach well ahead and to bear the dog's weight alone as the rear legs are brought forward. Most dogs are able to shift from one lead to the other during the canter (Fig. 2-23). When a dog changes lead it looks similar to the kind of skip you might make if, while marching

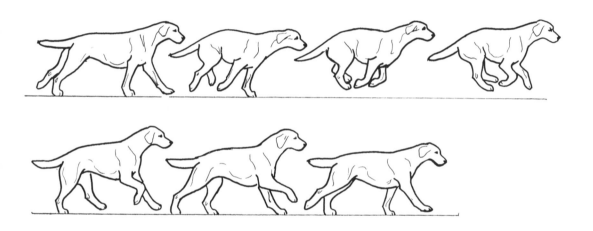

Figure 2-23. This dog is changing leads from left (top) to right (bottom).

with a band, you were to find yourself out of step with the others in your row. During jump training, it is essential that dogs be taught to jump using either leg as lead because there are situations where it is safer and more efficient for the dog to use one lead rather than the other. For example, when a dog is turning to the right, it is better for him to lead with the right leg.

The final on-ground adjustment is **bouncing** jumps. This is desirable in flyball competition in which extra strides between jumps slow a dog down and waste time. Bouncing jumps can also be a useful technique for a dog to use when two jumps are situated close to each other in agility. To bounce a jump, the dog must have excellent spinal flexibility. The dog must hyperflex the spine upon landing with the front feet, bring the rear legs forward to be placed on the ground ahead of the front feet, and then extend the front legs, straighten the spine, and extend the rear legs maximally to achieve the thrust needed to clear the next jump.

We bet you didn't know there was so much to jumping! We continue to be amazed at the ways that dogs can accommodate to different circumstances when jumping. They truly are phenomenal athletes!

Quick! What jumping style is this dog using?

3. The Complete Jump Training Program

This program will work with you and any kind of dog to improve upon what Nature gave you both. It is divided into three sections, each calling for a higher level of understanding and ability than the last. Each Level is a prerequisite for the next.

Please glance through this chapter first to get a feel for its philosophy and progression. Before beginning a lesson, learn the first several steps in order. That way you'll be able to stay a step ahead of your dog even when he makes rapid progress. It will also get you thinking, and in every section you should be able to come up with additional variations custom-tailored for your dog by you, the one who knows him best.

At the end of each section is a checklist to measure your dog's competence with the skills of that Level. This helps you assess how you've done with the lessons in that section and lets you pick out any skills that need extra attention.

Those working with dogs who are further along in their training should use the checklists to make an honest assessment, skill by skill, of your dog's level of understanding. Test the skills on the equipment, not just in your head! Most dogs picking up the program at Level II, for example, will have a few items from Level I that still need improvement. You should address those issues before advancing to the exercises that use them in the next Level. Shortcuts now mean gremlins later.

Level I - Foundation

It never hurts to start at the beginning, but it often hurts to push too fast. Obviously, some dogs will progress through the steps of Level I faster than others, and most will need extra work here or there. That's just a normal learning curve.

Many dogs who need extra time on a tough step end up being more reliable with that skill than the dog who seems to be a quick study. This happens as a result of the handler's patience, and it's a good investment in long-term confidence. Be willing to help the unsure dog understand and enjoy all the elements of a difficult skill at this foundation level; your patience will pay off. You control your dog's jumping career. Don't jump off the learning curve, and don't give up!

The ABC's of Level I
Attitude, Basics, Coordination

Attitude

The first requirement is the most important. Without a good attitude, talent is useless (the world of dogs, like the world of humans, has an ample supply of talented no-accounts). On the other hand, you may know an unlikely dog who has been very successful at the sport of his choice. A positive attitude can overcome many shortcomings.

In order to do our best, we must find the work rewarding. With dogs, as with humans, the reward is an individual matter. Anything we enjoy can be a positive reinforcer^. You must let your dog be the judge of whether something is reinforcing. When we advise you throughout the book to use a cookie for this or that, what we are really saying is, "Use a positive reinforcer appropriate for your dog at this moment." When we tell you to entice your dog, we really mean, "Bribe him shamelessly with a positive reinforcer that he finds irresistible." When we say to reward your dog, we mean, "Reinforce your dog immediately after he completes a behavior you like." That may mean anything from calling out "Good!" at the instant he clears the jump to rushing right in to interrupt the lesson with a cookie or a game of tag. You'll need to develop quite a cache of reinforcers for your dog, and you'll need to know your dog well in order to choose the right reinforcer for the moment. Attitude is nurtured by thoughtful reinforcement; not by constant overtreating long after the behavior is established and not by taking increments of progress for granted.

A good attitude is the proper first step in the development of a confident jumper. It's also the proper first step in the training of everything that requires teamwork between you and your dog, from attention span to work ethic. To get the most from any dog sport, you would be wise to begin with one thought in mind: attitude comes first. Long before the lessons are learned, your dog's attitude toward the sport has been shaped. Are we having fun yet?

Basics

The basic skills for jumping are not difficult, but if they're neglected they can simply become foreign to the dog. He will develop other, less efficient and less accurate, ways of handling his body over jumps. The beginner dog or puppy can avoid common bad habits and develop a lifelong love of jumping right here in this chapter. The dog with jumping problems generally belongs here too. Here he can dismantle his worries and reprogram his way of going over jumps. This will also improve his confidence for the sport in general, and therefore his attitude will improve. Everything is interlinked.

Remember, you choose the goals, but your dog decides what is easy and what is difficult. Learn to read him so he can show you what is needed and what works. The best trainers are continually learning from their dogs.

Coordination

Considering how often we humans trip over things, it has to be tricky to handle four feet at once. But some things are the same with four legs as with two. For example, your dog doesn't have to be looking down at his feet to be watching where he is going. Both humans and dogs negotiate their steps depending on an initial quick assessment of the terrain. Unless it seems complicated, the first glance is enough, and the eyes look forward or several steps ahead, not directly at the feet. Dogs who have a lot of experience with uneven terrain (those who go for walks in the woods, for example) quickly become skilled at negotiating obstacles on the ground. The more uncertain your dog is of the footing, the closer to his feet his eyes focus.

Level I Foundation Exercises

Step 1. The Ladder

There is no better tool than the ladder for helping your dog understand how many legs and feet he has and how to make them all work together. Use an extension ladder (compressed) for most dogs, or a wooden rung ladder for puppies and very small or timid dogs.

With one hand in your dog's collar and the other hand holding a cookie in front of his nose, simply invite him to step between the rungs. Spend your cookies according to how your dog feels about this weird contraption (a tidbit for each forward step if it's difficult; only occasionally if he's comfortable). Give lots of praise as he walks forward.

On this and every step, practice with your dog on the left and also on the right side. You don't want to turn jumping into a ritual. It needs to be a concept. Don't use the command word "heel" or any other valuable ritual word. If your dog wants to stare at your face as if in attention mode, put the cookie to his nose and entice him to face forward. Help him understand that this is not an obedience exercise. This introductory work should be quite relaxed and casual. In fact, don't even name the obstacle until the dog enjoys it and is beginning to understand the job. Until then, just entice him to participate in a new nonsensical game. No pressure.

It's a real plus, especially for a large, young dog, to have a helper on the other side who can wrap an arm around the dog's behind and touch his ribcage on the other side. The helper's near hand rests on the near side of the ribcage, and the forearm touches the haunches on the same side. We call this the connecting arm. It helps the dog steady his rear. You are helping him understand that he is all one body. If the dog won't allow a person to do this, a leash or ace bandage will suffice.

Remember that it's the ladder and the stepping forward over the rungs we want to reinforce. Spend your cookies in the ladder as your dog steps forward. Don't just feed cookies after the dog has exited. If he should choose to exit over the side, ignore that. Use the connecting arm approach, or simply try again if he wants to. If he's happy, he'll go further and further along until he's doing the whole thing, as long as you reinforce forward movement of the legs over the rungs.

But what if... If your dog is frightened, let him watch from the side while a more confident dog walks through the ladder getting treats. Model a happy attitude, and praise the other dog while he's working. If you're well coordinated yourself, some hesitant dogs will follow you if you straddle the ladder and walk backwards while enticing them. Some dogs are happy to follow another dog through. Some dogs do well if you pick them up and place them in the ladder, close to the exit end, so they only have to step over a single rung to get out. Spend a cookie when you put him in the ladder and one as he takes that forward step. When that goes well, you can place him with two rungs to go, etc. If you progress one rung at a time, you'll have your ladder obstacle solved in about 5 minutes. If you go from a rung or two to the whole thing, your dog may panic. Remember, attitude is everything here.

If your dog is eager and careless, stepping here, there, and everywhere, we have some favorite tricks. First of all, this is a nice problem because attitude is on your side. Usually you can control the feet with the cookie; you release a tidbit as soon as all four feet are in the ladder. You control speed by moving the cookie slowly forward, even backing it up if the dog tries to jump ahead. Another trick is to have a helper on the other side of the ladder so the two of you form a chute at the dog's midsection. That helps him stay in the middle. The connecting arm described above can help, too. Sometimes this kind of dog just has no clue where his body parts are.

Step 2. Ground Poles

Now that your dog is familiar with his body parts and how to coordinate them consciously, you can expand that skill on the training ground. Lay down a sequence of about 10 poles (jump bars, PVC pipe, 2x4 studs, etc.), each at least 5' long. Lay them on the ground approximately parallel to each other, like rungs on a giant ladder. This is called a straight-line sequence or a jumping lane. The poles don't have to match; a variety of materials is best. They shouldn't be evenly spaced but should be amply spaced, so your dog takes at least a step or two between each pole (Fig. 3-1).

Figure 3-1. A jumping lane consisting of parallel poles, unevenly spaced.

What?! Not evenly spaced?!! That's correct. It's important that your dog not perceive jumping as a ritual. He needs to become comfortable leading with either the left or right leg. Even if he chooses a favorite lead leg as his training progresses, he'll still be competent with either, and this will definitely make him a more capable jumper. The inevitable inconsistencies of jumping tests in the future won't phase a dog who has handled them all along. This step is to help him learn some elementary stepwork at the trot.

Have your dog trot on a loose leash down the line of poles. There's nothing scary about poles on the ground to a dog who understands ladder work. If your dog seems hesitant, walking rather than trotting is fine initially. If your dog chooses to go around the poles rather than over them, that is very important information for you. Review the ABC's and Step 1. Then go back to using one pole, then two, etc., with lavish praise.

As soon as your dog is comfortable and not hitting poles or looking underfoot, add more poles and change the spacing; keep the spacing varied but not tricky. Keep the leash loose throughout these steps to allow your dog free movement of head, neck, and spine.

Although it's not essential, trotting over the poles with your dog may be helpful and gives you a feel for the coordination you're trying to teach him. Just be sure to give him plenty of room — don't take the middle of the poles for yourself! Work your dog on both sides of course, and then get out of the lane entirely. You'll want to dispense with the leash when your dog is comfortable. It's fine at this step for you to trot down the lane beside the poles, praising your dog's efforts in the lane and monitoring when to complicate his job further. But in addition to switching sides, you should also vary, even if only slightly, just where you are in relation to your dog so you can avoid the common problem of accidentally training him to stay exactly beside you. He'll soon need to begin thinking of jumping as his own job. Put the leash on again briefly for a major variation such as Step 3.

Step 3. Quicksteps and Angles

Now it's time to introduce a bit of tricky stepping. Rearrange the poles, setting some quite close together, so there are spans with ample spacing and sections that require mincing steps over a few poles. Small dogs won't be so cramped but will still have to keep alert. On with the leash! Once or twice down the poles, praising your dog's accuracy, is all it should take to make your dog comfortable and smart with this. Now you're free to vary the variables such as the leash, your position, and the number and spacing of poles.

Next, change some of the poles by pulling one end this way or that (Fig. 3-2). The dog should still trot in a straight line, but some of the poles will be angled. Again, put him on leash the first time or two. As he learns to take this in stride, angle more poles and more sharply. Mix up the angles.

Figure 3-2. A jumping lane with angled poles.

Here your dog will learn that it takes a different perspective to negotiate a straight line of travel down a lane of odd-looking poles, and that a longer stride is required to accommodate a wider space. In figuring out these new twists, your dog may trot more slowly at first, but will soon handle them with no concern. Don't criticize him for tripping over a bar. Give him an opportunity to try again, allowing him to experiment with different ways of going. Praise especially as he clears a pole that previously fooled him.

You have quite a few variables to manipulate now, including leash, handler position, spacing and angling of poles, pole decorations, rewards, distractions, substrates, when you practice (use heat and weather conditions as additional variables), and where you practice (this system is quite portable). Coming up next is another important variable: jump height. From here on, your nimble dog will begin to show you some talents unique to his being a dog, an animal with quick reflexes and great dexterity.

Step 4. Height

Put aside the extra poles now, so you're back to 10 or so, parallel and variably spaced; no tricky footwork required. Now introduce a little height to the program, a maximum of 4 to 6 inches for little dogs and 6 to 12 inches for big dogs. Don't make everything the same height; you don't want to program your dog rigidly.

A delightful tool to use at this step is cavaletti, the ingenious little contraptions invented about 100 years ago for developing physical and mental coordination in horses. The unique advantages of cavaletti include portability, stability without stanchions (uprights), and adjustability to three different heights simply by rotating the base. Adapting the basic design for use with dogs allows for many possibilities in materials and construction. Our favorite interpretation is shown in Chapter 4 (Fig. 4-2). We strongly recommend a width of 5' in order to maintain an inviting, roomy look to the obstacle even when the poles are placed at angles.

For this step, use some poles on the ground and some raised, using individual broad jump boards, cavaletti, or standard jumps with low uprights. Bricks and blocks can be used to add height to your ground poles. We have even used soda cans, laying them on their sides and pressing a PVC pole into them. This keeps a round pole from rolling away and gives a jump height of about 3 inches. You can find articles to create just the right introductory height for your dog, too. (Note: Tall uprights and wings^ interfere with leashes. Introduce these variables only after your dog is off leash.)

When your dog is happy and comfortable with this new element, you can bring back the tricky stepwork and complicate the job again. Also begin to decorate your jump stands, or put something unusual beside an occasional pole to help your dog learn to ignore extraneous material and focus on the pole.

One position variable you'll want to play with is that of calling your dog to you over the jumps. This is not a formal recall, of course, but just another variation for your dog to master. A helper can steady your dog at the start — this is preferable to your worrying about whether he will wait until he's called. It's helpful for you to step over the jumps yourself, which encourages your dog to follow that path. Go only as far as you feel your dog will come down the lane; you can lengthen the recall as another variable in your personal training regimen.

Don't make everything the same height! Everything low is a good guideline for now, but everything the same will create problems later. Eliminate the tricky stepwork for your first few recalls, and let your dog enjoy running to you while negotiating the basic, uneven, low jumps. There are many good tricks to help your dog enjoy jumping this way, including any combination of these:
- running away from him as he's coming over the jumps.
- calling him from part way down the line and racing him to the end.
- throwing a toy ahead for him to chase.
- backing up while holding out a jackpot of treats as he runs to you.
- calling out his favorite "come and get me" invitation as he runs.
- causing a happy commotion: waving your arms, praising raucously, dancing with glee as he runs to you, etc.

This step may show you some interesting things about how your dog's mind works. In fact, observing a dog over multiple runs down a lane can be more informative than running one's own dog because you can see so much more of the dog's footwork when observing from the side. Does he come at a trot over a short distance and at a run over distances of 50 feet or more? We hope so. Does he leap over two poles close together? That's okay. It shows that he's alert and able to deal with them. Every reaction contains important information. Is he happy? Does he understand? Is he coordinated? What is he telling you?

But what if... Does he hesitate or go around or stutter-step anywhere? Make it simpler immediately, and work back up. There are lots of variables to change in order to make the job easier. Here's a short list; you can think of others:
- shorten the distance. Jump part of the sequence, then gradually more, beginning with the easiest section. (A retractable leash is helpful if your dog is familiar with it; first at short distance, then longer, etc. It's to show him the way, not to punish him if he tries to go around!)
- lower the jump heights.
- isolate the difficult part for separate practice. Break the exercise down into steps.
- make the footwork less tricky.
- review Steps 1-3 with lots of rewards until he loves every variable.
- use a helper to hold and focus the dog.
- have a helper run alongside with the dog on leash.
- any combination of the above.

Step 5. Jumping Circles
In Chapter 2 we explained how the canine athlete takes advantage of his dexterity and spinal flexibility. Now that your dog has a good deal of body awareness, he'll enjoy learning to maneuver in this simple configuration of low jumps or cavaletti (Fig. 3-3a). Use about six jumps in a circle, like spokes in a wheel (see Chapter 4, Lesson 5). They should be spaced fairly evenly at first, but that won't last long!

Working off leash, stand in the middle of the circle and invite your dog to trot over the jumps in either direction. Praise him for accepting the assignment and interrupt him occasionally to offer a reward. In a jump circle, the distance between the jumps depends on whether the dog jumps close to the inside or the outside of the circle. Your dog should be allowed to experiment with this and choose his own radius. Because he has some experience with stride adjustments and is by now very self-assured with this kind of work, he should soon settle on a comfortable rhythm. It will be useful later for you to note the spacing of the jumps in his chosen path. Be sure to work in both directions. Does he seem to have a preference? This is also worth noting (see Chapter 6 and Chapter 7). Give yourselves several sessions to explore this even spacing before complicating the job.

The circle can be changed in diameter, and it can be made more complex. One interesting game is to remove any two jumps to let your dog stretch further and perhaps change gaits in the larger spans between some jumps. Your dog will learn how to choose good take-off spots when turns are involved, as they generally are in agility and obedience. Then you can put those two jumps elsewhere in the circle, so there is a mix of generous and tight spacing (Fig. 3-3b). Does your dog restrain or extend his trotting strides, does he canter the open spaces and trot the tricky ones, or does he extend his canter to stretch over two tightly spaced jumps at once? His choices aren't right or wrong; they are interesting. They tell you about his personal jumping style.

The most advanced use of the jumping circle uses a wide diameter (20 to 30 feet) and asks for a continuous canter. The dog's inside front leg should automatically be his lead leg. When you call him to you and ask him to reverse directions, he should change leads. This is likely to be automatic for him too, as soon as he figures out the game. If at any time he is not on the inside lead, just interrupt him cheerfully and ask him to start again. Praise him for picking up the correct lead. He needs to become quite dexterous with this, and he'll soon learn that the inside lead is always the more comfortable. When you get to Level II, with call-offs and call-backs, this nimble balance will be the cornerstone of some very pretty teamwork.

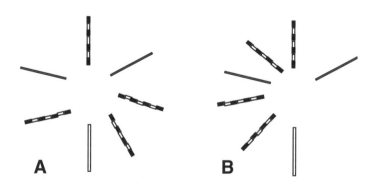

Figure 3-3. Jumping circles.

Checklist for Level I

1. Does your dog express interest when watching other dogs negotiate ground pole sequences? Is he eager when it's his turn?
2. Can he trot happily over a straight-line sequence with poles spaced unevenly? Eyes up?
3. Can he trot in a straight line over angled poles? Angled poles spaced unevenly?
4. Does he accept poles of different sizes, lengths, and materials without seeming to notice? Can he accommodate various low heights happily?
5. Does he happily work on various substrates: gravel, grass, wet grass, matting, plastic, carpet, frost, or snow?
6. Can he trot and canter rhythmically off leash over a circular sequence of jumps spaced evenly? Can he adjust when they're uneven? Does he automatically pick up his inside lead at the canter and change leads when he changes direction in the circle?
7. If he happens to hit a bar in the sequence, does he try a different strategy over the same sequence next time? Without losing confidence?
8. Can he accept weird decorations on the jumps? Can you position yourself anywhere along the jumping lane without disturbing him?

And another thing: Repeating foundation lessons later on is a good insurance policy because it reinforces important skills and reminds you and your dog how to relax as a team. People who never look back at the basics are putting their own egos before their dog's education. It's not a moral issue for your dog, so enjoy every step, whether it's your first time through, or just a review, and above all, if you're retraining to correct a bad habit. Repetition is the key to learning for all of us, so make sure the ABC's of Level I jumping stay fresh in your repertoire. This is your foundation: maintain it well!

Level II - Skill

Quick! What are the ABC's of Level I? Don't come here without them! This level is built on that foundation.

Here in Level II is where you and your dog turn basics into real skill and turn talent into mature, quality work. You can work up to regulation jump height here. Level II also introduces teamwork. (See Chapter 7 for a more involved discussion of teamwork for agility, including the TLC elements: Trust, Leadership, and Confidence.) As you add the ABC's of Level II to your repertoire without sacrificing the ABC's of Level I which you've patiently nurtured, you'll see a lovely teamwork begin to develop between you and your dog. Enjoy!

As throughout Level I, you should work your dog on both sides to keep him ambidextrous (and to make you more than a one-sided handler as well). Remember, too, that every team needs a captain, and that should be you. The captain trains hard to better his own skills as well as helping his teammate improve. What are your own strong and weak points? Try to isolate problem areas and devise ways to make yourself a better teammate.

Level II contains elements that can be demotivating if you lose your patience. In Level I you developed a fun-loving, forward-thinking dog who enjoys jumping and feels good about himself. Those good feelings can be either cemented for life or broken into bits by the way you handle yourself in Level II. Look at it from your dog's perspective: what's it like training with you?

The ABC's of Level II
Accuracy, Brakes, Control

Accuracy

In this level, your dog will learn to jump what is actually there to be jumped instead of just launching his body in a pre-programmed way. Jump heights often change by a bit here or there depending on equipment, terrain, etc., so keep your dog thinking at this stage. Give him lots of experience with different variables. He will get better and better at sizing up the situation and handling any jump without undue concerns about spacing, background, course difficulty, etc. It's up to you to keep his mind alert rather than putting him on automatic pilot. Accuracy is a critical skill if you ever want more than a rote jumper.

Our rule about jump heights is that you should treat increased jump height as a separate and important element of difficulty, proportionate to the size of your dog and his jumping prowess. This means that each of these Level II steps should be done first at low height and with other variables introduced before raising the jumps. Should the jumps be all the same height? No. Help your dog develop accuracy so that you can live with imperfect ring stewards, equipment, and conditions. How gradually should you raise the jump heights? Your dog is telling you. It is up to you to be honest in your assessment and remain tuned in to your dog as you progress. You're the one training him, and good training is two-way communication. What is he telling you?

Brakes

Running and quickstepping are fine, but can you stop him? Can he stop himself? Your informal recall in daily life is a good place to practice this skill. You will need a first-rate informal recall in this Level, because you will need to call your dog off when he's running full-tilt toward a jump he wants and you don't.

It's also time to begin teaching your dog to read your body language. Any competition where dog and handler are a team relies on body language, though some sports, such as obedience, require that our bodies speak quietly. Even where excessive body language is a no-no, you and your dog rely constantly on subtle body cues to communicate. The carriage of a hand, the placement of a foot, even standing straight and still are all body talk. We begin the training using more motion to make our directions understood, and we quiet our signals as the dog understands. Your ultimate goal probably requires working without a leash, too, but that doesn't mean that you should do without it from the start. It's one of many useful tools, especially for teaching brakes. We advise that every handler begin these Level II exercises with exaggerated body pivots and signals. We wean from excessive body talk the same way we wean from food or the leash or anything else: gradually, by "varying the variables." You and your dog will improve your teamwork by doing these exercises.

We begin teaching quick turns and body-talk skills with an exercise called informal attention. As we progress in this Level, we'll introduce unexpected changes of direction and quick pivots which require astuteness, good brakes, and four-wheel drive.

Control

Not that jump, *that* jump! The trick is to get cooperation without making control a dirty word. You won't have to sacrifice attitude to get control if you sneak in the control step by step, preventing mistakes rather than criticizing them. Your dog needs to be obedient no matter what your sport, but if he's not also thrilled to be on your team, you're missing the best part. What's it like to be trained by you?

Speaking of control and dirty words, please understand that we don't advise jerking on the leash! The leash is to prevent misunderstanding and miscommunication between you and your dog while you are both learning new skills. The sight of the leash should make your dog happy. The value of the leash is twofold. First, it puts the work into slower motion. That way, you're free to dispense treats and fine tune your footwork without losing your dog's informal attention. Second, it tells the dog in advance which way he'll be turning. He is experienced enough not to argue with the leash. It cues him for the call-off and call-back commands by his attention to keeping it slack. Enticing and rewarding your dog should be your interactive strategy. Punishing with the leash would only be harmful here.

Level II Skill Exercises

Step 1. Informal Recalls and Informal Attention

With or without jump training, the informal recall needs to be a well-honed part of your life, but you need it especially in competition jumping. Will your dog leave a strong distraction in order to come right away when you call? If not, perhaps you need to fill a pocket with cookies and put your dog on a long line amid distractions, or refresh some early shaping steps to his enthusiastic recall, or enroll in a noisy obedience class for the opportunity to brush up. (See Chapter 4, Exercise 3 for more hints on developing a great recall.) We are not talking about a formal position exercise. The informal recall means, "Interrupt what you're doing and come to me at once." You may even send your dog off in a new direction just before he arrives. This recall skill is the basis for all of your directional control in jumping.

Another cornerstone of complex jumping teamwork is informal attention. The dog does not have to be continually staring at you; that would be counterproductive. He needs to look where he's going and handle demanding jumping tasks. He should, however, be aware of your whereabouts, your actions, and your voice. That is not hard for a dog, with his superior peripheral vision, hearing, and his ability to keep one ear on you. All it takes is his desire to know what you might do next and his interest in being part of it. This skill is tied to bonding and to leadership.

Informal attention can be taught on leash with a handful of cookies and an interested dog. With the leash slack, just invite your dog to walk casually with you. Say something nice as you're walking, and when your dog looks up, pivot sharply as if to dart away, praising all the while and popping your dog a cookie the second he turns toward you. It takes only a couple of seconds and is done in one smooth motion. The idea is to pique your dog's interest in anticipating your next sudden move, then reward him for doing so. It's a game, and you're setting your dog up to win. Soon you'll see a confident gloat come over your dog's face, an expression that says, "Ha! You'll never fool me, the Wonder Dog! I can win this game!" Naturally, he's right. We are completely out of our league playing games of reaction time with canines. That's the point. You, the team captain, need to be able to take advantage of the quickness of your teammate, and you can only do so if he is paying attention.

In working on informal recalls and informal attention, as with cementing other behaviors, it's important to begin varying your variables one by one after your dog has learned the game. For example, repeat the exercise more than once before giving a treat, practice off-leash, in different situations, amid different distractions, at varying distances, etc. And, of course, bring the learned skill to basic and then more complicated jumping contexts.

Step 2. Call-Offs and Call-Backs

A call-off requires the dog to resist the next jump and to come out of the jumping lane toward you when you call him. A call-back requires the dog to turn around and repeat the previous jump(s). Both depend on the Step 1 skills, and both require timing and body language cues from you.

Perhaps your dog is now a more talented jumper than you are a handler. Don't let that discourage you. Just consider yourself a good trainer, and practice your part without your dog until you feel proficient. Borrow a human to be your practice dog if you want another intermediate step. After all, you break your dog's complicated jobs into many learning steps. You deserve the same patient approach. You may also want to introduce call-offs and call-backs with your jumping lane in a simple mix of ground poles and slightly raised poles, then gradually challenge with heights, angles, etc. Otherwise, feel free to keep your higher heights from Level I, but begin with ample spacing so as to ensure enough room for your dog to resist traps and turn comfortably.

To **call off**, begin by running alongside the sequence while your dog jumps, and surprise him with a recall to either side at any point (Fig. 3-4). The goal is to teach your dog that you may change the task at any time and that it's a game to see if he can respond quickly. Make sure you set him up to be successful at first. The foolproof way to do this (always a good choice for the first time) is on leash, backing off the lane in an exaggerated way as you call your dog and praise him for turning. Call early, when your dog is in the air over the previous jump, rather than when he lands. Reward lavishly! Remember to begin praising when your dog turns toward you, not just when he catches up to you. It's his decision to turn that you love.

59

To **call back**, create a big gap between any two jumps in your straight-line sequence; this is your designated turn-around space (Fig. 3-4). Run beside your dog and alert him to turn around and go back the way he came. Praise as he turns. This can be rude if you don't give him time to absorb his momentum and change direction 180 degrees to begin jumping again. Good timing on your part and a strong upper body pivot will help your dog to turn tightly and quickly. You have to be commander, coach, and cheerleader all at once. But it's a lot of fun when you and your dog put this skill together.

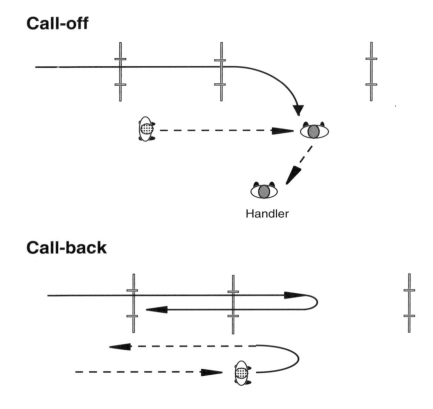

Call-off

Handler

Call-back

Figure 3-4. Jump patterns for call-offs and call-backs.

But what if... If your dog keeps on going, or seems confused, don't worry about it, but don't let it happen again either. Put him on leash right away and talk him through it to make sure he understands the interruption when you call him. Resist the urge to get angry that your fast dog is "blowing you off." After all, going forward and jumping gladly is hardly a terrible problem at this stage. It shows that your dog has confidence and loves the work. Just smile and try it again on leash. Also work on Step 1 skills several times a day, away from the jumping lane.

Step 3. More Height and More Variation

Remember that as you raise jump heights, you'll need to provide proportionately more space between jumps. And don't forget to vary all your other variables as well. It's most important to keep your dog's confidence high and to prevent him from becoming dependent on inappropriate cues. If a pattern develops, your dog will find the pattern, even if you don't recognize that it exists.

Some patterns are good, like praising him when he gives you a brilliant new attempt or quickly rewarding each repetition of a new skill until the behavior is established. But other patterns can be detrimental, like forgetting to skip the food reward now and then once the behavior is established, or using always the same single reward in your repertoire instead of varying the reinforcements (look at the list of rewards to choose from for the recall over jumps in Level I, Step 4, for example). Some common variables that you need to vary at this step include:

- where you stand when you begin the exercise, and how you move.
- the call-off and call-back spots, and whether you call at all.
- the jump heights, angles, and spacing.
- the dog's direction of travel (from one end, or from the other).
- rewards and how often you give them for well-learned behaviors.
- the appearance of the individual jumps (also interchange their positions).
- training locations, substrates, weather, time of day, companions.
- noise and other distractions during familiar challenges.

There are other, potentially more important, variables, some of which only you know to be important for your dog. Take advantage of how well you know him and prepare him to overcome weaknesses (both yours and his).

Step 4. Wavy Lanes, Serpentines, and Figure 8's

Now we depart from the straight-line sequences. Wavy lanes are jump sequences that curve irregularly, and serpentines call for a smooth, slalom-type path. Put your dog on leash and practice negotiating low jumps and poles in different shapes such as those in Figure 3-5. These examples are only to get you started — vary your placements with more or fewer jumps, different spacing, add an occasional solid jump, etc. Spread the jumps out at first to give you both room to maneuver. This may feel more awkward for you than for your now highly-coordinated dog. These exercises will help you and your dog learn to switch sides gracefully and turn smoothly to either direction. Use the leash to guide your dog to cross^ in front of you in the middle of the figure 8. (This work is taken further in Chapter 7.)

Aren't we done with the leash yet?! Let's discuss the leash as a training aid. The leash can be very useful at this Level without being a negative tool. Think of it as a familiar guidance, a means of showing your dog the correct response while preventing a myriad of incorrect responses. That's the problem with teaching things like changes of side and tricky jump sequences — there are too many unfamiliar elements of difficulty being attempted at once. The leash can let you get your own footwork and bodywork coordinated with your dog's by putting the act in slower motion while you're both learning to change sides (or to do other intricate maneuvers).

Serpentine

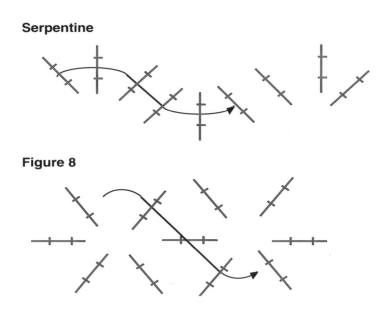

Figure 8

Figure 3-5. Serpentines and figure 8's

The leash also relieves the dog of responsibility for directional control and speed. For the insecure dog, this eliminates a good deal of worry, and he can therefore concentrate on learning the information without feeling the pressure of guesswork. For the brazen dog, the same leashwork has a calming effect on mind and body, enabling the dog to look at the elements of the job we want him to learn. In either case, the leash lets you isolate the element of turning in motion, showing the dog how to coordinate his movement with yours.

After your dog can perform serpentines and figure 8's on leash, he can begin to learn a new set of signals sent by your shift in body position as you indicate a new direction. It won't be long before he can read you on the run, no leash required. Because of your patience and patterning with the leash, he will also desire to do so and will respond appropriately. So don't categorically dismiss the leash at this stage. It can help you and your dog put some fancy footwork together, and those skills will help you read each other's body language in any sport.

Step 5. Three-Jump Sequences

You and your dog can practice difficult approach angles, changing sides, call-offs, call-backs, and send-aways without having regulation equipment or a generous amount of space. Figure 3-6 demonstrates some well-known three-jump configurations. Each of them can be worked in a small space and can be run in more than one way. Got five minutes? You can have a terrific jump training session: lively, useful, and fun. Review your ABC's regularly to keep your sanity about jump heights, etc. A new skill requires lower jumps and perhaps a leash at first.

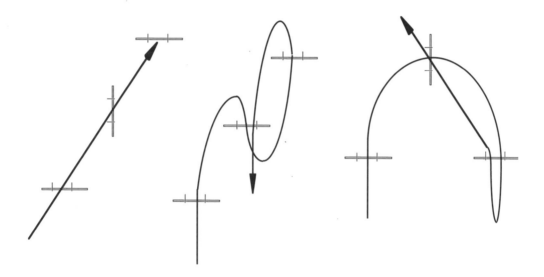

Figure 3-6. Three-jump sequences can be used to practice call-offs, call-backs, and send-aways.

Step 6. Four-Jump Sequences

Working with four jumps is especially useful when you're ready to introduce traps, which are obstacles (in this case, jumps) positioned so as to be inviting when a different one is requested. Figure 3-7 shows some favorite configurations. There's nothing magical about them; you can think of many more, as well as more ways to use these setups.

Just one thing before you start doing more complicated sequences: it's not fair to start on your mini course without a game plan. A dog's reaction time is so much faster than ours that even our best timing is not up to his reflexes. You want him to learn to read your body language, so don't let your body give him garbled messages. If you do make a mistake, just relax and praise your dog. There's time to beat yourself up later if you must. Your confusion or frustration might frighten an insecure dog, or it might incite a mutiny in a busy dog. If you're not sure what you want to do next, work it out in your head without your dog. Be sure of yourself when you direct him, or at least act that way.

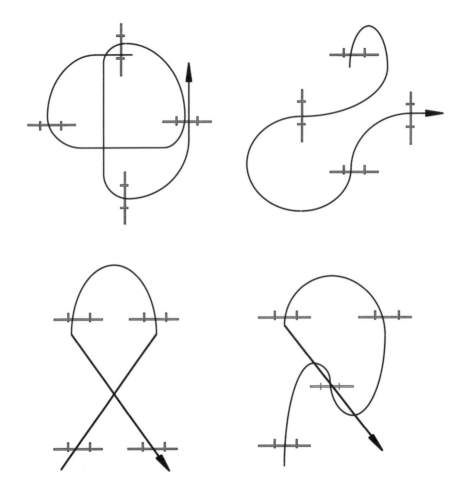

Figure 3-7. Four-jump sequences can be used to introduce traps.

Step 7. Spreads and Broad Jumps

Spread jumps, also called oxers, have considerable depth as well as height. They may be specially-made units that support two or three jump poles, or they may be fashioned by standing two or more single-pole jumps together, one behind the other. Spreads may be parallel, so that the top poles are both at the same height, or ascending, with the front pole being lower than the back pole (Fig. 3-8). The back pole defines the jump height. Broad jumps (also called long jumps) are extended jumps which are low to the ground. Instead of poles, their jumping surface is a series of slightly ascending, angled planks. Their biggest challenge is in the long stretch required to clear their distance.

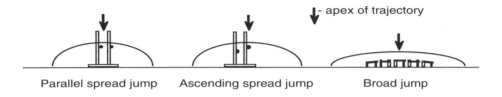

Parallel spread jump   Ascending spread jump   Broad jump

Figure 3-8. Spreads and broad jumps.

You should fashion several downscaled spread jumps using whatever supports you have (bricks, cavaletti, cement blocks, soda cans: see Level I, Step 4). Make them low and highly visible, with ascending rather than parallel bars at first. As with other jumps, avoid patterning to an exact set of dimensions. The height of your highest bar should not present any challenge to your dog, but it's as important as ever to vary the height early on. As an upper limit to start, the highest bar should be a maximum of your dog's elbow height.

By now, you should be able to judge what is a good height at which to start your dog, and you should be a good observer of what your dog tells you by his reactions. Take your best initial guess (err on the conservative side), try it out, and ask yourself if it was a good guess. What parameters should you change to give your dog early success? Then experiment and have fun from there. The trajectory your dog will ultimately use over a spread is only slightly different from that of a single jump of the same height; nonetheless, the spread certainly looks different. Enjoy, and let your dog enjoy, all sorts of low ascending spreads so that he can experiment, too. This helps him find and expand his **comfort zone** for spreads. The comfort zone is the area in which he is safe launching his body to clear the jump. He needs to get a feel for the comfort zone. No amount of theory or handler interference can substitute for his own experience.

Dogs who are introduced to full-height spread jumps too quickly tend to enter an unhappy cycle of misjudging a spread and then losing their comfort zone, making it hard for them to experiment and become fluid again. You can prevent that. If your dog misjudges a spread jump at this Step, you should first praise him for trying, then help him to have success. You know him best. Should you let him try again or make the spread easier? Should you get out the fish treats? His favorite toy? Should you do motivational recalls over it? Should you go back to Level I, Step 4, and gradually introduce baby spreads there? A jumping error is not a tragedy; it's part of the learning curve. But repeated errors or loss of attitude should alert you to change your approach.

One measure of your dog's progress with low ascending spreads is whether the apex of his jump trajectory occurs over the highest bar. That means he's reading the jump correctly and taking off within his comfort zone for that height. Much more on this is covered in Level III, but we mention it here so you'll begin to help your dog find and expand his own comfort zones. You'll then come to Level III with a dog who is adaptable and able to handle difficult jumping challenges. So please, set up many different low spread jumps for your dog to enjoy and experiment with, but don't tell him exactly

Photo by Mary Jo Sminkey

Figure 3-9. This Norwegian Elkhound clears the broad jump with more horizontal than vertical stretch.

what to do or when to take off. If you continue to work gradually and avoid patterning him, he will expand his scope as a jumper, developing a wide comfort zone and remaining accurate.

To introduce parallel spreads, which are harder for the dog to judge than ascending ones, gradually reduce the height difference between the front and back poles of your ascending spread. When you're ready for both bars to be the same height, begin by offsetting one bar to the side slightly to aid the dog's perception. The apex of your dog's jump trajectory should occur midway between the first and last poles of a parallel spread, so this trajectory is not so very different from jumping a single vertical jump. Some handlers choose to give the spread jumps a separate name from the single jumps. That is for you to decide. The broad jump is also named separately by most competitors, to alert the dog's focus to the ground.

For taller dogs, the broad jump is eventually jumped with more horizontal than vertical stretch (Fig. 3-9), but short dogs have, proportionately, a more difficult job. The broad jump can be as high as a spread for them, making it doubly challenging. No wonder they tend to walk on the boards! Plan to take extra steps here for small dogs, rather than introducing both elements of difficulty (height and length) at once. One well-known trick is to turn the boards on edge initially, to make the obstacle look more like a jump than a platform. But often, that creates a dog who jumps upended boards and hops onto flat ones. What does that tell you? More intermediate steps are needed to get from upended to flat (you knew that!). Our favorite solution is to add a bar jump, which already evokes the thought of jumping. Start with the pole low over the middle of one or two broad jump boards, depending on the size of your dog, and gradually move it toward the back of the obstacle to encourage stretch.

Likewise, if your obedience dog loves the broad jump and you'd like to introduce spreads for agility, start off with the jump height low, make the bars more visible by ascending the heights from front to back, and place a couple of broad jump boards underneath to make the new challenge more familiar.

As you increase the height of your spreads and the breadth of your broad jumps, your dog will learn to recognize them and put out the extra effort to handle them. Don't require a sharp turn immediately upon landing after either of these wider jumps until your dog is fully mature, strong, and well-coordinated. It's too hard on the inside shoulder. But as soon as your dog is comfortable with a certain spread, that spread should be incorporated into a simple jumping lane. That will expand the contexts in which your dog can handle spread jumps and broad jumps. He's getting to be a very smart jumper.

Checklist for Level II

1. Does your dog come instantly when you call? Even when he's distracted?
2. If you run with your dog on a loose leash and you suddenly turn and run the

other way, does he think this is an exciting game? Does he win?

3. Can you call your dog off a jump which he expects to take? With a smile?
4. When your dog is running a straight-line sequence of jumps with you running alongside, and you suddenly pivot and turn around, does he turn too?
5. Can your dog maintain rhythm and accuracy when the sequence curves? Can you and your dog switch sides when the sequence turns sharply?
6. Can your dog handle angled approach sequences in a straight line? Off leash? At a canter?
7. Does your dog know how to jump a spread jump? A broad jump? Does he enjoy them? How can you tell?

And another thing: At this level, it becomes more important for the dog to have time off to let the learning sink in. It's a well-studied phenomenon that both rest and sleep are periods when learning seems to gel. The sleep-learning ideas (and jokes) stem from experiments done decades ago on all kinds of animals, including humans and dogs. It seems that more complicated tasks are learned better if a period of rest, particularly sleep, closely follows a training session. (That also implies that if your dog had a very unpleasant training session, he may internalize aversion rather than cooperation. His attitude is still your doing!)

LEVEL III - Power

In Level III you get to bring it all together, knitting a closer bond than you have ever felt with your dog. But there aren't any shortcuts to readiness for this section; you have to earn it. So answer honestly: what are you doing here? Did you leap over the other sections and land here? Many good dogs have had the fun of jumping pressed out of them by doing that.

This is where your dog learns to see the big picture. It's an opportunity for growth for you both as individuals and as a team. As team captain, it's your job to be alert for signs that your dog is sore or otherwise not up to strength. Power work requires a power body, so make sure your dog is lean, fit, and warmed up before sessions. Use the flexibility exercises and your repertoire of games to ready your dog's body and mind, and your own, for a work session (see Chapter 5 for guidance).

Above all, keep your sport and your training in proper perspective. You can't solve a single one of the world's problems with your jump training today.

The ABC's of Level III
Altitude, Brains, Concepts

Altitude

First and foremost, power jumping is not for all dogs. It is only for the strongest, soundest, fittest, and most confident and athletic dogs. Don't be disappointed if your dog shouldn't be jumping extremely high. There are many things you can take from this chapter, but major altitude may not be among them. We are not going to lecture you on fitness and soundness here, but more than ever, it's important for you to keep your dog safe.

At this point height becomes a major factor, a separate element of difficulty to be reckoned with under pressure. We want your dog to have a feeling of strength and confidence about jumping now, so much so that if you were to raise a jump in the series to a few inches higher than he had ever jumped before, he still would clear it, because he cannot be fooled about how high something really is. He sizes it up in a split second on the approach, and is so comfortable with his body and ability that he simply gives an extra bit of lift for the higher jumps.

Brains

The tricks of power jumping go beyond physical ability. Power thinking requires attitude, talent, focus, and experience. When your dog is capable of this kind of thinking, he can see the big picture of a course, taking in the general feel of it from the start line. Is this a Jumper's course? Open or Utility obedience? He can tell within seconds of entering the ring. The power jumper carries a wide intelligence for the sports in his life. And he loves to jump.

Power thinking requires skilled training which allows your dog's analytical strengths to develop. The foundation is laid in Levels I and II, where his mind is challenged and encouraged, his mistakes ignored, and more correct responses skillfully shaped. In this section, you and your dog will be working hard on teamwork as well as skills. Many dogs will be decisive enough to make many mistakes, and how you react will depend on your dog's temperament. It's important not to punish him for thinking any more than you should be punished for trying yet another new idea. You and your dog will both need to do some experimenting here. With patient guidance, your dog will develop a working mindset extremely compatible with your own. The two of you seem to communicate telepathically; you read each other perfectly and respond to each other appropriately, with respect and affection and zest for the job at hand.

Concepts

By now, your dog should be a concept jumper. Your chosen sport will require some rituals and some concepts, but jumping should always be something your dog is intimately familiar with. You won't need long lessons to introduce him to a new twist in jumping, and most of your new twists now consist of team efforts between you: how to handle a tricky course sequence together rather than simply how to introduce your dog to a new skill. A five minute lesson can introduce a new point for you both to ponder.

Level III Power Exercises

Step 1. Flatter Trajectories and Greater Speed

Hopefully you've done a great deal of experimenting with spacing in your jump series throughout Levels I and II, so your dog knows how to extend and collect his stride. And hopefully you've laid the groundwork in positive control with all of your Level II skills. Now you can fine-tune your dog's ability to flatten his trajectory and soar.

Your dog is ready for all sorts of demanding challenges, but you must have a game plan before you start working your chosen sequence. Here are a few examples:

1. Ask him to jump at full speed down a lane of full-height angled jumps set quite far apart (20 feet or more for large dogs).
2. Add some waves to your straight line jumping lanes so that he has to go out of his way to jump them all (Fig. 3-10). He should show a preference to soar over, rather than go around, the jumps.

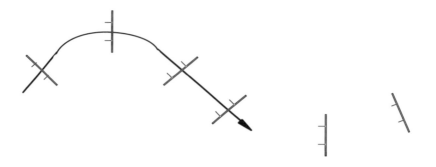

Figure 3-10. Widely spaced jumps forming a wavy lane to practice developing fluidity, flatter trajectories, and greater speed.

3. Put greater distance into your serpentines and other configurations (see Level II for just a few possibilities), so that your dog can combine full speed with his quickstepping talents at higher heights.
4. Replace one or more of the jumps in a lane with long broad jumps (increase the length gradually, and don't overdo it). This is a great way to get your dog to stretch out over jumps. If you run alongside initially, or throw a ball for him as he's clearing the jump, it will help keep him thinking long and low.

It is best for the dog to jump no higher than is necessary to clear the jump because doing so is harder on the body and takes longer. The time it takes to jump depends on the height to which your dog elevates himself, not the height of the obstacle.

Remember, power jumping is not for all dogs. This is not the best way for an overweight dog to jump (and most dogs are overweight by our standards). But a lightweight, fit dog can take off further away from the jump and use extra power to propel himself further in the air in less time than it takes a heavier, less fit dog to canter closer to the jump, take off in a rounder arc, land closer to the jump, and get up to speed again (Fig. 3-11). Both dogs spend the same amount of time in the air, but Dog A has covered about three times the distance in that time. He has also saved ground time. Dog A is airborne while Dog B is cantering closer to the jump, and Dog A has landed on the run by the time Dog B even leaves the ground. Obviously it takes more power and speed to take off sooner and clear the jump. But the effects of gravity are the same on both dogs — it will take both dogs the same amount of time to elevate themselves to the high point of the trajectory and to fall back to earth.

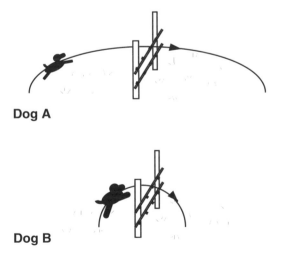

Figure 3-11. Dog A takes off further from the jump and uses extra power to propel himself further in the air in less time than it takes Dog B to canter close to the jump, take off in a rounder arc, land closer to the jump, and get up to speed again.

Dog A

Dog B

Power trajectories are appropriate for sports like agility, flyball, and Schutzhund, where speed is appreciated, but they have limited value for obedience, except for dogs small enough to benefit from a full head of steam in the confines of the ring.

Step 2. The Comfort Zone

As mentioned earlier, the comfort zone is the area from which the dog can safely take off to clear a jump. Better jumpers have larger comfort zones. By teaching your dog to be a concept jumper rather than a ritual jumper, you will greatly expand his comfort zone. The power jumper has the largest comfort zone. He also has an effortless way of adjusting his stride to place himself at his preferred take-off spot (PTS^). That spot varies in its location depending on his assessment of the big picture, but he's not dependent on being at his PTS. His jumping talent gets him out of a pinch time and again. He makes jumping look easy.

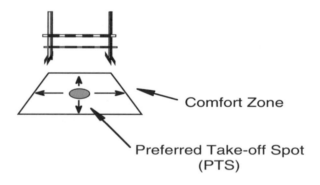
Comfort Zone

Preferred Take-off Spot
(PTS)

Figure 3-12. The comfort zone and preferred take-off spot (PTS) for a specific dog and this particular jump. Note that the comfort zone and PTS are mobile; they expand and shrink and move to different locations depending on the circumstances.

The most important thing to remember about comfort zones is how individual they are, so be careful not to force your idea of the correct comfort zone onto your dog. Comfort zones differ greatly from dog to dog because of the many factors that affect athletic ability. A dog's comfort zone is a function of (in alphabetical order): age, angulation, attitude, experience, health, jump height, strength, structure, talent, training, and weight.

Somewhere within your dog's comfort zone is his PTS: the location at which he'll try to place himself for take-off if all conditions are favorable (Fig. 3-12). Just as the comfort zone varies widely from dog to dog, so does the PTS. Your dog's PTS and comfort zone should move further from the jump with increased speed and closer to the jump with increased jump height.

To a lesser extent, it should vary from one type of jump to another (see Level II, Step 7). Dogs who lack experience with a variety of jump presentations sometimes have comfort zones no larger than their PTS. If you have progressed with us from Level I, it's likely that your dog's PTS is approximately in the center of a large comfort zone, even at his regulation jump height.

Even the power jumper's comfort zone gets shorter and narrower as the jump gets higher, because more of his effort goes into vertical lift, leaving less strength available for the horizontal component of the trajectory. Some dogs can jump with a flat trajectory over a 30" jump, but no dog jumps flat over a 6-foot wall.

This means that the higher the jump, the more carefully the dog has to pick his take-off spot. The better athlete, though (or sometimes the better *trained* athlete), will always be able to clear the height from a larger comfort zone than the inferior, or careless, athlete. Having a larger comfort zone means being able to be less precise about the take-off spot, which is a big advantage since it's difficult to be exact while on the move. More important, it means being more likely to overcome a misjudgment or an unexpected complication, like poor footing or a bad angle.

Step 3. Measuring First Jump Set-up Distance^ and Working Stride Length^:

Different sports require different stride lengths. For example, every jump in obedience is a first jump, and there's always a first jump in agility and flyball. Because strides for a first jump are usually of a different length than those for subsequent jumps, it is important to measure the **first jump set-up distance**, the distance from the first jump at which the dog should be placed. It is also important to measure the length of a dog's strides in the middle of an agility run (called **working stride length**). Since there are many non-structural factors that influence stride length, it is most useful to measure it while the dog is moving. If your dog is not yet jumping regulation height, then take these measurements using the maximum height he is currently jumping, and remeasure when you get to regulation height because his working stride length will change.

First Jump Set-up Distance: This represents the distance away from the jump at which your dog can comfortably take two or three strides as he is accelerating from a sit to clear a jump. Your dog's first one or two strides are not as long as subsequent ones. This is a universal phenomenon attributable to inertia, so you can expect heavier dogs to take longer to get up to speed (even human racers using starting blocks take a few steps to get up to full speed). This explains why the first jump claims so many victims in agility. The inexperienced dog is apt to choose a take-off spot appropriate for subsequent jumps at full momentum but too far away for the first jump given his slower rate of speed on start-up. In other words, the dog needs to have a different PTS for first jumps than for jumps taken at full speed.

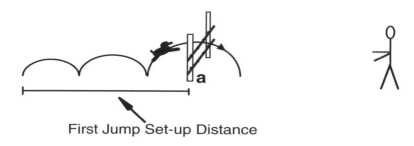

First Jump Set-up Distance

Figure 3-13. How to measure the first jump set-up distance.

To measure the first jump set-up distance, leave your dog in a sit approximately 20 feet away from a jump. Go to a point approximately 30 feet from the other side of the jump and call your dog (Fig. 3-13). The reason that the dog is called, rather than sent over the jump is that being called will encourage the dog to charge the jump, and this is what we would like to stimulate in training. The object is to allow the dog a minimum of two strides before taking off to clear the jump. Have a helper stand to the side of the jump to count strides and to observe whether the peak of the dog's trajectory was centered over the jump. If not, move the dog until it is. Then measure the distance to the jump. This is your dog's ideal set-up distance for a first jump. The first jump set-up distance may need to be altered to include more or fewer strides for different circumstances. For example, you may prefer that your dog take three strides before the first jump in agility, but there may be only room in the obedience ring for two.

Working Stride Length: This represents your dog's stride length when he is in the middle of an agility run, going at a comfortable speed. The working stride length for a given dog in agility is usually longer than that of the same dog in obedience. Note that in flyball, your dog's stride length is pre-determined because of the desirability of bouncing the jumps. Set up a jumping lane using two jumps approximately 20 feet apart. Put a small piece of brightly colored tape on the top of one of your dog's front toes and have a helper stand on that side of the lane. Walk to a point approximately 30 feet from the second jump and call your dog. The helper's job is to note the spot on the ground where the taped foot lands on the second full stride after landing from the last jump, and run to mark it — we use a golf tee outside and tape inside (Fig. 3-14). Measure the distance from the jump to the mark, and divide that number by 2.5 to get your dog's working stride length. If your dog works inconsistently, you can repeat the exercise several times and take the average stride length. Note: Your finding constitutes the working stride length for *this* dog, at *this* speed, over *this* jump height.

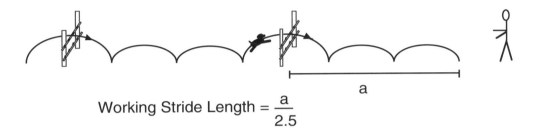

$$\text{Working Stride Length} = \frac{a}{2.5}$$

Figure 3-14. To measure your dog's working stride length, call your dog from about 30 feet beyond the second of two jumps placed approximately 20 feet apart. Have a helper note the point at which one of the front feet touches the ground on the second stride after landing. The distance from that point to the jump, divided by 2.5, is the working stride length.

Your dog's working stride length serves as a baseline distance from which to calculate the spacing between jumps for the improvement of skills designed to make your dog a more resourceful jumper. In addition, a knowledge of your dog's working stride length will help you choose the most appropriate path for running an agility course. In addition to shortening with decreased speed, your dog's working stride length will shorten in deep sand, hot weather, slippery conditions, when running uphill, or when he lacks confidence. When you are using your dog's working stride length to calculate the ideal distances between jumps for a given training exercise, adjust them according to the parameters of the day. Get into the habit of noticing how your dog copes with the different jump spacings he encounters. This is the only way to become an expert about your own dog's work over jumps; no amount of theory can do that for you.

Step 4. Bounces, Extra Strides, and Half Strides

A bounce is the absence of a stride between jumps; the dog lands after one jump and immediately lifts off again for the next jump. Extra strides are called for when a jump is further away than expected. And half strides are choppy, shortened strides inserted when the distance between jumps is too short for a comfortable stride and too far to bounce. There are times when your dog will need to use each of these techniques in order to clear jumps. Every sport has them: a poor dumbbell throw, a nasty agility sequence, a dropped tennis ball, etc. In this step, we will also discuss the lengthening and shortening (extension and collection) of working strides. Because of the strong foundation you have already provided your dog, he has met each of these challenges at lower heights, so this Step is a logical progression for him.

As your dog has progressed through his jump training, his individuality as a jumper has matured, too. By now, you should be familiar with his strong and weak points, but take time to learn his personal preferences as well. There are many athletic dogs who will naturally bounce full-height jumps in a series at 12 feet apart. There are other good jumpers who never bounce if they can fit in a half-stride. Though you'll want to educate your dog in these techniques to make him a better judge of jumps, you don't need to coerce him to specialize in one approach or the other unless it's important for your sport. As a general guideline, obedience competition benefits more from half-strides and collection; flyball benefits from bouncing and extension; and agility benefits most from extra strides and extension. You can help your dog become proficient in each of these skills, and then allow him to choose when to use which one.

Bounces, extra strides, and half-strides won't be difficult for a dog who has dealt with unpredictable spacing all along, and you can set up specific exercises to hone each skill. Remember, when you set up jumping sequences with the intention to leave 1½ stride lengths between jumps, allow ½ stride each for take-off and landing space, for a total distance between jumps of 2½ stride lengths. You should also consider the height of the jumps (since you wouldn't want to work always at regulation height), as well as the parameters of the day mentioned above. Remember that your dog's working stride length is a baseline, and exercise your judgment to adjust from it rather than forever taking it as unalterable. Your dog is as individual as you are.

As your dog becomes a more talented jumper, he will be more flexible about extending and collecting his strides while running. For example, he may be able to take two extended strides instead of 2½ strides or two ¾-strides rather than 1½ strides. This means that you may have to be more resourceful in order to work on half-strides. But you should practice them occasionally just to be ready for the day when he'll be faced with the unexpected need to insert one.

A half-stride can be coerced by starting your dog purposely at an awkward distance from a jump. Place him about ¾ of his ideal first jump set-up distance away from the jump. This should force him to fit in a half-stride (Fig. 3-15). Another way is to set a surprise jump at a right angle to the expected series, and call your dog to the new jump just as you practiced call-offs in Level II, Step 2. At first, the unexpected jump is low, and it's just ½ stride out from the jumping lane, so as soon as the dog turns, the jump is upon him. Don't forget to praise him, especially if he didn't care for the exercise. Important matters like enticement, reward, distances, and jump variables should be adjusted based on what he tells you with each jump.

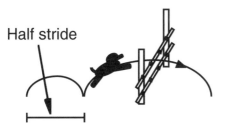

Half stride

Figure 3-15. To practice half-strides, set your dog up about ¾ of a stride length from the jump and send him over. The jump will be too far away to clear in a single stride and the dog will usually fit in a quick half-stride in order to arrive at his preferred take-off spot for the jump.

Encouraging your dog to take extra strides is much easier than teaching half-strides. To get your dog to take two full strides between jumps, place the jumps three stride lengths apart (this allows ½ stride each for landing and take-off). Proportionate to the quickness of your dog, allow enough room before the first jump to let him get up to speed. Then increase the distance between jumps to four stride lengths so that he learns to take extra strides between jumps (Fig. 3-16). As he becomes more proficient, vary other variables, including jump heights (does your dog's stride length shorten or lengthen as you raise the heights?), your position, distance to the first jump, number of jumps, use of angled and wavy jumping lanes, spread and broad jumps, etc.

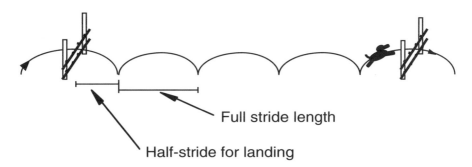

Full stride length

Half-stride for landing

Figure 3-16. To encourage your dog to take extra strides between jumps, place them at least four stride lengths apart.

Do you know at what spacing your dog will comfortably bounce two or more jumps in sequence without taking a stride in between? As a training exercise, bouncing is a great builder of strength and coordination throughout the body. As with all our other skills, it's not necessary to work very high jumps in order to learn the maneuvers. Placing lower jumps closer together is preferable. You can estimate the distance by initially spacing your jumps ¾ of a working stride length apart, which allows room for a modest landing and take-off, but no stride in between. If you don't know what to expect, you can remeasure your dog's working stride length using jumps at elbow height, or you can work from the following 'good guess' system.

Begin with a series of five or six jumps spaced at an average distance of 2½ feet for small dogs, 5 feet for medium, and 7½ feet for large dogs. All jumps should be at the same height for evaluation purposes — just below elbow height is a good place to start. Check for bounce and for comfort, which your dog will show you by the evenness of his strides and the happy look to his body. The purpose is to determine at what spacing he is most comfortable bouncing (Fig. 3-17). That distance is his baseline bounce distance for that height. His baseline will vary with jump height and will increase with experience, confidence, etc.

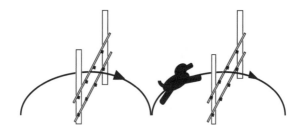

Figure 3-17. Bouncing jumps.

Note: We are not trying to regress to ritual jumping! It's just that the best way to work any one element of skill is to isolate that element and practice it alone for a bit, then bring it into other contexts. Do not spend many sessions with your spacings or heights identical.

As soon as your dog understands the bounce maneuver, begin to vary the spacings slightly to hone the skill. Other variables to manipulate include: working up to full height, adding the new skill to jumping lanes which incorporate more than one type of striding requirement, and incorporating the new skill into more complicated sequences. As you raise jump heights, your spacing may also need to increase proportionately, depending on whether you want to work on lengthening or on collecting his stride.

You can help your dog practice lengthening (extending) his stride, which will expand his comfort zone for bouncing and will also make him

78

more astute about adjusting on the run for oddly spaced jumps (lengthening two strides rather than inserting an extra half-stride saves time). Work from his most comfortable bounce distance and gradually increase the spacing between jumps. As you extend beyond his baseline, increase the spacing more and more gradually. When your dog decides to add a stride or half-stride, you have just exceeded his maximum bounce distance. Increasing the distance gradually prolongs his decision and gives your dog a longer maximum bounce distance, thereby extending his strides over the jumps. If you rush, your dog will add a stride between jumps sooner rather than later; that would shorten rather than lengthen his bounce distance.

You can help your dog practice collecting his stride using the same series of 5 to 6 jumps, but this time, raise the heights without increasing the distance between them. Your dog will need more impulsion for the extra height, but will have to control that extra power because he'll be constrained by the relative closeness of the next jump. Collecting his stride does not always require him to slow down; it can mean increased energy and impulsion spent more in vertical lift and less in horizontal distance.

Step 5. Easy

Every eager jumper needs a "slow down and be careful" word to prevent him from rushing pell mell into trouble. Teach this command on the flat (without jumps), and teach it on leash. Yes, on leash, even in Level III. There is no benefit to calling out commands on which you cannot follow through, and the leash prevents this from occurring. The leash allows you to bring the skill of "easy" to straight and wavy jumping lanes, serpentines, and more tricky jump sequences, slowing your dog down wherever single-step poles and jumps are presented. The leash also serves to remind you that even your advanced dog needs to begin at Step 1 with a new command. We all do.

The teaching phase of any command should be set up in such a way that your dog cannot make a mistake, and therefore can be introduced to the new guidance with cheerful and heartfelt appreciation for his cooperation. The fact that the responsibility for correctness falls mostly to you is beside the point. If you can get him to cooperate with the first step, you have the opportunity to make cooperation worth his while. As we know, that is the key to attitude, which leads to teamwork as well as compliance.

The leash allows you to control the learning steps in a positive way by eliminating many potentially disruptive behaviors before they even enter your dog's mind. That gives you the opportunity to use your vast repertoire of positive reinforcers with the quick timing and good nature that accompany a training session going smoothly. Your positive reinforcers should include the leash, which presumably your dog likes. It's a tug toy, an invitation to be with you, a cue for the informal attention game which he loves (see Level II, Step 1). The leash should not be demoralizing. If your dog dislikes the leash, then make sure it's associated with treats and fun and with being brilliant at new learning. Never use it as a punishment (and that includes putting it on only after your dog makes a mistake).

To teach the command "easy" on leash, invite your dog to trot briskly and casually forward with you, but don't use any ritual word. After a few steps, say, "Easy" and slide your nearest hand down the leash all the way to the collar, as you slow way down to a walk without stopping. What you want is a very pronounced slowing of the dog's pace, and your own. Praise (and reinforce with a treat if you like) as you both walk, and continue several steps this way. Then resume your brisk pace with an invitation word like "Okay!" or, "Let's go!" Repeat this exaggerated slowing down on "easy" about three times during your first session.

We know you know this, but don't forget to gradually vary your variables such as reinforcements, your position relative to the dog, gradually saying the command before you interfere with the leash (and recognizing and praising when the dog begins to slow down before you begin to slide your hand down the leash), speed of travel, distractions, weaning from the leash, introducing the well-learned skill to ground poles, stairs, low jumps, etc.

One good way to keep control as you gradually dispense with the leash is to practice "easy" with your ladder (see Level I, Step 1). Trot up to it, on leash if you like, and say, "Easy" as you get there. Praise the dog for slowing down to do the ladder (and don't worry about ladder mistakes here), and remove the leash in the ladder if all is going well. Continue "easy" just a step or two beyond the ladder, and then celebrate.

When it is time to bring this skill to tricky jump sequences, have your jumps low and build a real contrast into your jumping lane or serpentine; several jumps amply spaced followed by an intricate section which you anticipate by saying, "Easy" to warn your dog of upcoming quicksteps. You might want to be on leash for this at first, and have everything downscaled to accommodate your own brisk and slow paces.

You can think of more ways to advance your dog's understanding of this command without setting him up to ignore you. These intermediate steps are where many people lose control of a new command. After the concept is learned, use it in tricky jump sequences, first on leash and then off, gradually complicating the variables. Avoid the two most common pitfalls of the intermediate steps of this command. Don't give your command too late for the dog to respond. Its value is in telling the dog what to expect in the immediate future, so it needs to be predictive. Even more difficult, the intermediate steps require that you be prepared to interrupt your dog and repeat the command if he disregards your advice, so take advantage of different situations and practice setups once you're ready to take your new command on the road. "Easy" is a command that will go a long way toward guiding your dog through some difficult jumping exercises when he is especially distracted or keyed up. It can bring him back to you mentally so he can keep his act together physically.

Step 6. Occasional Bigger Jumps

If your dog is sound and strong, there is a place in your training — a small place — for jumping higher than regulation height once in a while. Not a whole series of bigger jumps, and not much bigger than regulation, but just enough to make your dog supremely confident at regulation height. There are two benefits to doing this:

1. Sometimes a jump that is set at regulation height will be taller in effort required. Many factors (sometimes related to human error, but more often related to the terrain or footing) can account for this. It's most common in agility classes, where the course layout might position a jump uphill (more power required at take-off) or downhill (more force on landing.)

2. Training past your dog's regulation level of difficulty is one of the best ways to maintain a high level of confidence for the regulation task. The pressure of competition is draining, and what looked easy enough in practice can appear daunting when it counts. Being prepared to jump even higher lets your dog feel safer under pressure. The height he sees in the ring will be lower than what he knows he can do.

This concept of preparing for an effort beyond that which is generally required, called overtraining, is abused so badly in the world of dogs that it requires further discussion. For some reason, it has become an all or nothing argument. Either people never let their dogs see a higher jump, or they ask for too many too often. So, before you go off and raise all your jumps, please read on...

Overtraining is a routine procedure in many sports, but it does not apply equally to all sports. Many sports contain challenges requiring long-term conditioning to ready competitors for a burst of maximum output which could not be sustained on a regular basis. Marathon runners do not routinely run marathons, Grand Prix horses do not routinely jump full-height courses, and Iditarod sled dogs do not routinely train over grueling distances. Instead, they all work many shorter courses in training for longer ones; they concentrate separately on strength, skill, and endurance, and nowadays, they also cross-train^. High-output athletes, be they human, equine, or canine, are trained carefully and piecemeal, not on a steady diet of overtraining. The harder the exertion for your dog on competition day, the more important are planned days off and strategic conditioning in preparation. Don't make a habit of hitting him with everything you've got, thinking you'll make him tougher. It's more likely that you'll hurt him in one way or another.

Overtraining for jumping will shorten the athletic career of all but the strongest, most lithe-bodied dogs. For jumping, being strong means being able to carry one's own weight effortlessly (like the marathon runner rather than the weight lifter). Along with general soundness and fitness, it's a low weight-to-height ratio that bodes well for a long jumping career (see Fig. 1-4). In general, dogs with a weight:height ratio of 4 or greater are in the danger zone, and jumping will be tough on them. Those with a weight:height ratio of 2.5 to 4 should be jumped only when the footing for take-off is good and the landing soft. Dogs with weight:height ratios of less than 2.5 suffer much less stress on the bones, muscles, and ligaments when jumping. Of course, this is only a guideline, since conditioning and attitude can provide leeway for this number. Julie's Rottweiler Jessy looked like she was made solely of muscle and wire during her 4-year agility career. She maintained a weight:height ratio of 3.0 — a lean Rottie, but heavy by our standards. A dog with a lower ratio could have competed longer, but Jessy was retired against her will at 7½ years of age.

Each dog has a finite number of big jumps in him. So, although teaching your dog to recognize and handle occasional higher jumps is a smart move, don't spend those expensive big jumps unwisely. And don't think you're doing your dog a favor by overtraining if you haven't kept up with your conditioning homework. Big jumps are only for dogs who are fit.

Overtraining is often confused with overjumping. If your dog's regulation jump height is 30" and you always practice at 32" as a margin of safety, you are teaching overjumping. Teaching your dog to overjump everything in hopes that he won't hit bars in competition is an example of ritual jumping, or patterning. It is not overtraining. Proper overtraining enhances your dog's expertise as a concept jumper. Patterning your dog makes him a ritual jumper, whether your jumps are always identically low or always identically high. Overjumping will make him less smart about jumping. On a competitive note, it also takes longer to overjump than to jump efficiently, an important factor for agility and flyball. An extra half-second times eight jumps is four extra seconds. Placements and titles are often decided by hundredths of a second.

Step 7. The Big Picture

All the skills you have worked on with your dog, and all that Nature gave you both, will come together to make you a solid jumping partnership. The simple commands to speed up and slow down, to go this way or that, will be internalized by your dog to the extent that he has learned them thoroughly. As your dog gains experience, he learns to read the big picture. In addition to responding to what you tell him to do, he learns to respond as the jumps dictate.

The skilled power jumper knows when to take advantage of his ability to tuck his rear up in order to negotiate a tight landing area. He learned in Level I to read the upcoming jump, and he learned in Level II to think ahead, but now he begins to develop a feel for large pieces of work. In other words, he can think farther ahead while handling the present situation. The flyball power jumper is able to retrieve an escaped ball and get back on his correct return path no matter where the ball landed or how awkward the angle back over the jumps. The agility power jumper is perhaps the most talented of all — he can stretch out and soar over wide-open jump sequences at more than five yards per second, then quickly tuck his rear and jump tightly through a more tricky part of the course, turning in mid-air all the while.

The value of power jumping skills for the obedience competition dog is in becoming extremely confident about jumping and being comfortable enough with variations so that potential snags like optical illusions (which we affectionately call 'obstacle illusions'), poor matting, cramped or odd spacing, uneven ground, inferior equipment, unusual distractions, bad weather, even handler error, can't get the better of him over jumps. He can just plain handle everything.

Checklist for Level III

1. Can your dog read your subtle body cues and change direction accordingly without stopping?
2. Can you read your dog as well as he reads you, and do what is necessary to help him?
3. When your dog makes a mistake, can you tell whether he's unsure of himself?

4. Does your dog have a large comfort zone for standard jumps? What about for ascending spreads, parallel spreads, and broad jumps?

5. Are you becoming an expert at breaking concepts down into steps for the purposes of teaching your dog new things or improving old skills?

6. Can your dog handle a series with one jump higher than the others? If he jumps a series that includes a couple of very low jumps, does he flatten his arc rather than overjump them? In other words, can he jump what is actually there (concept vs. ritual)?

7. Can he find the rhythm when it's there? Can he adjust his stride on the run as necessary when a rhythm is not there (extend, collect, extra stride, half-stride, bounce)?

8. Does your dog slow down when you ask him to? Even on the approach to a jump or during a series of jumps? Off leash?

And another thing... You can't be happy until you want the dog you have.

Enjoy!

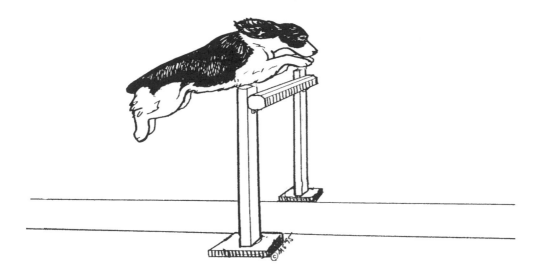

4. What About Puppies?

Let's get one thing straight before we say the words "puppy" and "jump" in the same breath. Puppies should not be putting the force of landing on the open growth plates of the front assembly, nor should puppies be straining the rear assembly by pushing off with power. So when we say we're introducing the puppy to jumping, it's the fundamentals he's learning, with the emphasis on FUN.

Puppies are perfect candidates for learning the ABC's of Level I of The Complete Jump Training Program (Chapter 3), with a few modifications. There is no better time to teach Attitude, and this chapter contains some puppy-minded tricks for developing it. There are several Basics your pup can learn while he is quite young and several games for improving Coordination as your youngster develops.

Many people are confused by the well-known statement that the puppy's brain is mature at seven weeks of age. That refers to studies showing that the EEGs (electroencephalograms, or brain wave graphs) of puppies at seven weeks of age are largely indistinguishable from those of adult dogs, whereas the EEGs of younger puppies register the immaturity of the neural activity in their brains. To oversimplify, around the age of seven weeks a puppy becomes capable of processing new information in much the same way an adult dog would process new information.

So should you train a young pup as you would an older dog, with the exception of physical challenges? Not a chance. A gigantic difference in ability to comprehend input separates puppies from normal adult dogs, because the puppy has been alive for such a short time. He has such limited experience at the new mental maturity level that it's impossible for him to have a meaningful frame of reference yet for new material. In other words, he may process new information like an adult, but for him, everything is new information because he's still a baby. And, being so young, he lacks mental stamina and easily overloads from too long or too intense an experience. He also lacks the ability to sort out which stimulus^ is the more important, leading to a stream-of-consciousness flitting from one attractant to the next. To the puppy, all these various stimuli may be of equal interest because he hasn't explored any of them enough to take them for granted.

A human child's EEG matures at about 10 years of age, yet the child still has many learning experiences ahead of him. Do you remember feeling overwhelmed by situations that you would later take in stride? Have you ever reexamined information as an adult that you had learned as a pre-teen, and found that you understand it better now that you have more background to bring to the learning task? Can you remember when you were learning to drive a car? It's quite a challenge to monitor simultaneously all the details of driving plus all the external variables (traffic lights, road signs, other cars, pedestrians, directions, conversation within the car, etc.) that beset us while we drive.

How do we become so comfortable with a complicated task like driving a car? It would be impossible if it weren't for the mind's ability to let the familiar become automatic. The young puppy, even with a mature EEG, is likewise bombarded with information which is extremely important to him. Along with increased exposure to the world comes familiarity, and along with that comes the ability to monitor familiar aspects of the environment automatically. At that point, the puppy may tend to ignore the familiar and become completely engrossed in whatever is novel. At this stage, the human partner has to work a bit smarter to remain interesting! Fortunately, jumping is one of the more complicated and most interesting things you will teach your puppy, so there's no reason to run out of training ideas.

As the puppy's world expands further and further, he becomes able to resist a pronounced shift of attention even when a new stimulus presents itself. That takes a lot of mental stamina. A good trainer, rather than demand prolonged full concentration from the inexperienced puppy, will use only a few planned **training sessions** but many brief opportunities each day to shape the puppy's focus, gradually developing the pup's mental stamina along with his repertoire of human-centered information. We call these very short exercises **training moments**.

The best time for training young puppies is whenever the pup is alert and interested in you: mealtimes, reunion times, and after naps, to name a few. A training session might last five or ten minutes, but don't underestimate the value of a training moment. It is these brief moments of opportunity interspersed throughout your time with the puppy that are most telling of the training bond between you. The effects are cumulative.

The more physically and mentally mature your puppy, the faster he will be able to move through the exercises in this chapter. But take time to enjoy the learning process, and keep attitude your highest priority. A puppy is young for such a short time! The younger he is, the greater a percentage of his experience is each training session and every training moment. Make sure each exercise is an investment toward years of enjoyment, not only in jumping but also in the pleasure of being together.

The exercises in this chapter were designed for the capabilities of puppies, to take advantage of their mental and physical eagerness without overtaxing their immature minds and bodies. This philosophy is just as useful in rekindling mental and physical eagerness for adult dogs, especially those who need extra confidence, or remedial work on Level I, or retraining for poor jumping habits. Have some fun with puppy stuff!

Training Moments

These tiny sessions last for seconds and pay very big dividends in bonding as well as training.

Exercise 1. The Touch Connection
Now is the time to accustom your pup to gentle handling all over his body, for three reasons: 1) so he won't be offended by polite body guidance in the future; 2) so you can relax him (and yourself) with touch when he's nervous; and 3) to begin to teach him body awareness. The puppy with a

good feel for his body grows up to be better coordinated, which is a big head start in jumping.

To establish this communication, work a little at a time, initially when your pup is napping and then just whenever it feels right. Start with his favorite spots (face, ears, tummy, rump) and work from there, over time, toward ticklish spots. Everything, including tail and feet, should be nurtured in this way. When invading a new or sensitive area, keep one hand based in the adjoining familiar territory and make small circular passes into the new area with the other. Also make sure to massage under and around your pup's collar. It's very important that he welcome hands coming to take his collar. Think of this as an exercise in trust. There are many books and seminars about the power of touch. Teach your pup to love massage, TTouch, Reiki, whatever you like.

Exercise 2. The Attention Connection

It's easy to teach your pup to pay attention to you. This quick game encourages relaxed eye contact and builds your image as the leader and the most important source of interesting activities in your pup's eyes. As your pup gets older, you may want to specialize in formal obedience attention or informal agility attention. The dog who can pay attention amid distractions will be a better jumper under pressure and a better teammate in any sport.

Take advantage of a moment when your pup is quiet and relaxed, perhaps settling down for a nap. Cup his chin in one hand, and with the other, touch his face just beside his eye, and then touch your own face beside your eye. Praise quietly as eye contact is made; hold only a second or two, then release with "Okay!" If your pup is stressed by cupping his chin, skip that part until he can accept it (see Exercise 1). Keep this a no-stress moment. Gradually lengthen and vary the length of gazing time. Soon you won't need to touch faces.

You can also do the attention connection another way. Practice both ways if possible. Choose a moment when your pup happens to look at your face, and praise him at that instant. Just smile and say a one- or two-second happy thing like, "Goooood," or "Good boy!" or "Hi there!" as your eyes meet. That's it. Don't stare at him until he breaks eye contact; that's the opposite of what you want. Better for you to be the first to look away. As his attention to your body gets stronger, you can further reinforce that tendency by inviting an attention connection just prior to playing a favorite game.

One caution to the owners of hard-driving dogs who tend to fixate on a certain object: reinforce attention on you, not the object of fixation. Don't throw the ball when the pup is staring at the ball. Use whatever trick you like to get him looking at you, and play the game he wants in response to that attention on you. At this young age, you have a much better chance of being able to teach your dog to refocus on request, and it's a skill that will serve you well later on.

Exercise 3. The Recall

There are few items on which experts agree, but here is one: the earlier you teach your puppy to come when you call, the better. For our purposes, the specialized jumping for agility, flyball, or obedience benefits from a top-notch recall. (Some prefer to teach two recall words, an informal and a formal one. The informal recall is the one we mean here.)

Many training books offer lists of games and gimmicks for stamping a reliable recall into your impressionable puppy's brain. It is preferable to use several different tricks in order to keep the command interesting and the context fresh. There are several good rules of thumb about teaching the recall:
1. Initially, call your pup only when you're sure he will come, and make him very glad he came.
2. Take advantage of important incentives like meals, car rides, treats, opportunities to go outside or play a game, and use your recall word when inviting your pup to these incentives.
3. When you want to give an untrained puppy some freedom outside, put a long line on him so as not to throw your recall away, and practice outside with enticements.
4. Praise your pup's decision to come, not just his arrival.
5. Practice in all environments, and use enticements again whenever a new context is introduced.

Exercise 4. Flexibility

It's tempting to do the same flexibility exercises for youngsters as you would for grown dogs because, if anything, the pups seem more flexible. Unfortunately, this is not the way it works. Although puppies are more rubbery in the legs and spine, you can harm them by cranking their bodies around.

But, assuming you'll be careful and conservative, it's good to have your puppy flex laterally in both directions, because dogs, like people and horses, choose a preferred bend early in life and tend to remain more flexible in that direction. Having your puppy flex to both sides also helps him become ambidextrous mentally and more resourceful with his body. You should also teach him to stretch his neck up and down. This improves flexion, strength, coordination, and balance through the neck and spine. Just let him follow a cookie or use massage to relax and stretch his muscles.

The most important thing to remember for puppy flexibility exercises is to proceed only one step at a time. Read the section on flexibility exercises in Chapter 5, and modify each one by limiting it to the first level of difficulty. As your puppy matures, he'll be ready for the more strenuous steps, one by one, and they will be easy for him because of the readiness work you do now.

Exercise 5. Wait

This means "restrain yourself," and it is an important piece of the control picture for jumping sports. An easy way to teach this is by holding the puppy back while placing an enticement on the floor and telling him to wait. Quietly prevent the pup from going anywhere until he gives up trying; then immediately say, "Okay!" and let him go. The quicker he holds himself back, the quicker he gets his freedom and the prize. This skill is different from the position-specific stay command which means "remain in that position and location."

The key is to notice when the pup is really holding himself back and to require this effort at first for only a second or two before releasing. After all, self-restraint is very hard work for a youngster, and we all know many adults who don't have a handle on it either. As your puppy learns to control his urges and wait for longer moments before release, begin to use this skill more generally; when going in or out of doors, for example. Remember to help at first whenever the learning context changes or new distractions are added. Once your pup has good control around the house, it's time to bring wait-training to your jumping sessions. Have a helper steady him at first! Even though the wait training and the ground pole training may separately be coming along smoothly, putting them together still constitutes a change of context. Don't risk weakening either skill or dampening your pup's enthusiasm with a correction.

Exercise 6. Doorways

An easy way for your puppy to get many extra baby jumps in a day is for you to put a very low barrier across a doorway. This might be nothing more than a cardboard cylinder threaded with string and tacked into the molding. Other adaptations range from a scrap of lumber or PVC to a tension rod or chin-up bar secured at a height of a few inches. Almost anything will do, the idea being that the puppy trots over it so often that the negotiation becomes automatic and comfortable. Remember, you are working on things like attitude, timing, and coordination rather than strength, power, and courage. First things first.

Training Sessions

These lessons last up to 5 or 10 minutes. Remember to stop before the puppy tires, so he's eager for next time.

Lesson 1. The Ladder

What does a ladder have to do with jumping? It has to do with being aware of all four feet and coordinating the lift and drop of them consciously. Walking is one thing that has become automatic for the pup, so the purpose of this exercise is to remind him about the elements of movement. He'll need to know how and why to control his legs in order to be responsible for each of them as the stepwork gets more tricky. A wooden rung ladder laid on the ground is generally a good height and spacing for this exercise. Read the section on ladder work in Chapter 3, Level I, to familiarize yourself with handling tips and 'what if' contingencies.

Lesson 2. Ground Poles

The big difference between ground poles for pups and ground poles for adults is the complexity. Puppies should be introduced to poles amply and unevenly spaced (Fig. 4-1), and the distances and set-ups should be changed regularly (see Chapter 3, Level I), but the quick-stepping and tight, fancy

Figure 4-1. Watch for the tail-up, happy stepping attitude that lets you know you are building attitude.

footwork which the mature dogs can rapidly master should be left for later. Enjoy letting your pup discover angled poles and happy recalls over several poles. Nothing need be more than pastern height to teach him all he needs to know until his legs are strong and developed.

Lesson 3. Signals

Signals are useful in many dog sports, and they teach your dog to watch you for clues. Puppies are quick to pick up the concept of signal training because their minds are open, and they tend to look for leadership outside themselves while they're young. Along the way, your pup will also learn about target training, which has lots of positive transfer to jumping sports like flyball, obedience, and agility. This is one good way to teach signal and target work and to incorporate them into your jump training.

A good foundation in wait-training is beneficial here. Face your puppy and have him wait while you place an enticement about two feet to one side. Send him quickly as you signal with your whole arm, almost but not quite touching the enticement. The idea is to gradually make the signal more subtle and move the target further and further away, until your puppy, perhaps months from now, will charge on faith to a target he hasn't yet spotted, taking his directional cue from your signal.

There are many variables to play with in this exercise, including size and type of target, distance, strength of signal, presence or absence of a verbal command, and working both directions. We don't recommend incorporating more than two choices of direction until your pup is older, but we do recommend adding a ground pole between your puppy and the target as soon as he's very good at the game. Nothing challenging *per se*, not a high or scary jump, just a minor complication that requires thought and coordination.

Lesson 4. The Send-away

A lovely opportunity to introduce the concept of send-aways presents itself to you every mealtime. Many obedience training books recommend teaching the puppy to focus ahead to the dinner bowl (nice application for wait training) and to go to the bowl on command and/or signal. This step can be begun while the puppy is quite young. It is easier to do jump send-aways with pups who understand signals already and who have a bit of mental maturity, so this is for older puppies who need another complication after learning about the signal exercises in Lesson 3.

Because this is a new twist, don't just pick up where you left off on the signal work! Step 1 of the send-away might look like this: stand beside your puppy, with a target set a few feet in front of you, and send him ahead with a strong signal just as you sent him to the side when he was first learning. Though this seems easier than the dinnertime send-away your pup already knows, the change of context makes it a good place to start. Naturally, increase the distance gradually and change the variables, as with the signal work. Add a ground pole, then another, to the send-away. If you've done your homework and not rushed your puppy's training, this is really going to be fun. To see adolescent puppies begin to combine mental and physical coordination skills with teamwork is exciting and rewarding. Remember to keep each session short.

Lesson 5. The Wheel

This is especially fun in puppy kindergarten class, where puppies can learn to follow one another over the spokes of the wheel (Fig. 4-2). Spaces between the poles get larger as the puppies work further out from the center, so bigger and faster youngsters can use the outer edges to avoid being cramped. This design also makes it easy to change the spacing for puppies by positioning them differently, without having to move the equipment, an advantage when working with a group. Initially, handlers stay to the outside or the inside of the wheel, or simply walk over the poles beside their puppies. Of course, as you already know, it's very important to work each puppy in both directions.

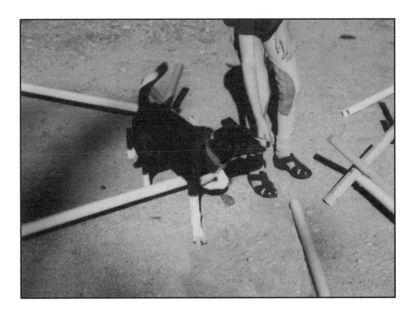

Figure 4-2. Working the wheel with a 4 month-old puppy. Smaller puppies can work closer to the center where the poles are closer together, while larger puppies work closer to the outside.

One good exercise for a puppy who is experienced with various placements in the wheel is to have him spiral inward, which effectively makes the stepwork progressively tighter (Fig. 4-3). Be sure to include spirals that turn in each direction. The spiral game also requires pups to work over angled poles, because the approach angle to each pole is canted toward the middle. As your puppy becomes comfortable and proficient in the wheel, you can vary the design. Change the diameter of the wheel, the number and placement of poles, your own position, etc.

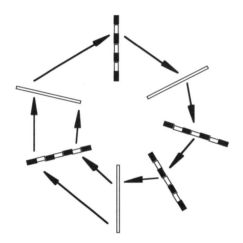

Figure 4-3. The spiral teaches the puppy to alter his footwork on the move. As he gets closer to the center, he needs to use tighter footwork. The spiral can also help him experiment with using different lead legs.

Lesson 6. Sequences

After your puppy understands fairly complex ground pole series, expand his mind with other challenges interspersed with the poles. For example, teach him to trot over a noisy plastic tarp, through puddles of water, through a tunnel fashioned from a cardboard box, etc. Many of the obstacle games described in the puppy chapter of *Enjoying Dog Agility: From Backyard to Competition*[1] would benefit your puppy no matter what adult goals you have for him. These downscaled challenges single out different areas of mental and physical development. As your youngster integrates all these different skills and learns to call them up appropriately, he's becoming smarter. He's learning how to enjoy solving problems, so he'll be a partner who can accept the unexpected and think on his feet. Slowly but surely, he's becoming your working teammate. This is how innocently a work ethic is nurtured. May you never stop developing your canine athlete in this positive, gradual way.

Reference
[1] *Enjoying Dog Agility: From Backyard to Competition*, J. Daniels, Doral Publishing, 1991.

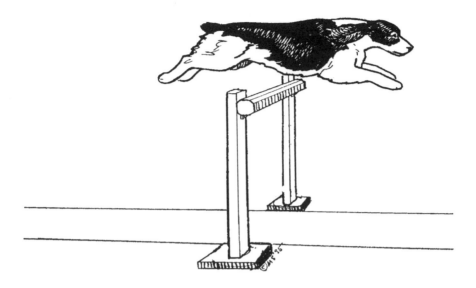

5. Conditioning
The Canine Athlete

For performance dogs, as for human competitors, fitness includes both physical and mental conditioning. The physical and mental components of competition depend upon each other in proportion to the intensity of the endeavor. Your dog can be in fabulous physical condition, ready to handle demanding tasks one after another without tiring, but he's not ready to handle a strenuous day of competition unless he also has the mental stamina.

Many of us have seen the dog who is full of beans outside the ring but, after stepping across the threshold of the ring, walks as if his feet are made of lead. That is none other than mental stress expressing itself physically. Likewise, all the mental toughness in the world won't get your dog through a demanding day of competition if he doesn't have the physical strength to hold up.

When we were children, our dogs were physically fit for any sport because they played hard with the neighborhood kids for hours each day, racing the outfielders for the long fly ball, pulling kids on roller skates and ice skates. Our dogs were involved in everything from trail riding to badminton, with all the energy and the glorious free physical expression of children. They had more than their share of conformational faults, but they had incredible body awareness, strength, coordination, and flexibility. They were way ahead of sports medicine in demonstrating the value of cross-training. And wow, could they jump!

We believe in working dogs up to fantastic physical fitness before jumping them high. The further removed a body part is from ideal structure for jumping, the more attention you need to pay to putting that part of the body in great condition. Julie's Rottweiler Jessy was certainly an unlikely dog for agility, but she had an outstanding competitive career full of many "firsts" and "onlys" at the 30" jump height. Years after she was retired she is still lean and strong, enjoying agility. (At ten years she earned her Junior Handler title at the 18" jump height.) Her lifelong physical fitness has to be part of her good health now.

This chapter will show you some new ways of thinking about canine conditioning and give you the tools to invent additional exercises that suit your situation and your goals. Many of the conditioning exercises in this chapter are designed to make your dog smarter and more mentally resilient as well.

If you are pursuing an athletic endeavor with your dog, you need to make regular exercise a high priority. Exercise is the element of wellness most often neglected by conscientious dog people today. Unfortunately, for many well-loved competition dogs, their sport is their only major exercise. Conditioning your dog for sports can be loads of fun, and it's also your responsibility. Your dog needs to be strong enough to do what you ask of him without overtaxing himself. If he isn't strong enough, then you are hurting him. The strain may show up in an injury today, or it may weaken your dog for the next time, but you will not get away with it forever. Make an honest assessment of your dog's physical condition with your most strenuous sport in mind, and begin a well-rounded conditioning program right away.

Before Starting

Just as you would not recommend that an overweight man who has not been to the doctor in years begin to run five miles a day, so you should not start your dog on a strenuous program of training and conditioning without evaluating his structure, level of fitness, and health status. This is even more important because your dog can't (or sometimes won't) tell you if he is hurting, especially if the activity is fun!

Structural Assessment

Before beginning a conditioning program, it is essential that you objectively evaluate your dog's structure and his current state of fitness and health. Use the information in Chapter 1 as a basis for an assessment of your dog's structure. Decide first whether he has an ectomorphic, mesomorphic, or endomorphic body type. Measure his weight and height, and see where he lies on the curve in Figure 1-4. If he is to the right of the curve, he tends to be ectomorphic (lighter weight for his height) and will have an easier time jumping than most other dogs of the same height. If he is to the left of the curve, he is more endomorphic (heavy set) and will have to exert more effort in jumping.

Next, evaluate your dog's front and rear angulation. Then make a list of your dog's strengths and weaknesses (for no dog is without both). Use this list to create a conditioning program unique to your canine teammate.

Fitness Assessment

You should also evaluate your dog's current level of fitness. To do this you must ask yourself two questions: 1) Is my dog at a correct weight for performance? 2) How strong are my dog's muscles? Whether a dog is being prepared for the obedience ring or the Iditarod, it is essential that canine athletes be maintained at a correct weight. In many breeds, for a dog to win in the conformation ring, he must be fatter than is healthy for long-term performance in other sports requiring real strength and endurance. Excess weight increases the stresses on the musculoskeletal system regardless of the performance event. How can one determine whether a dog has excessive fat? The best way is to test three different parts of the body: the neck, the ribs, and the hips. As in humans, individual dogs may carry the majority of their weight in one particular area, so it is best to check all three areas.

1. To check the neck, press your thumb and index finger deep into the side of the neck just ahead of the shoulder blade and pinch them together, making a tent of skin. Then pull your pinched fingers away from the body, letting the fat below the skin slip through your fingers. There should be no (or only a minimal amount of) fat.

2. To check the ribs, place your thumbs on the middle of his spine half way down the back, and run your fingers over his

last few ribs. You should be able to feel the bumps of his ribs without pressing in.

3. To check the hips, run your hand over your dog's croup (the area over the pelvic bones). You should be able to feel the bumps of the pelvic bones that lie on either side of the lumbar spine without pressing down.

Some of you may be reading this and thinking, "I would never want my dog to be that skinny!" Think about Olympic athletes. Picture the track and field competitors such as Carl Lewis or Jackie Joyner-Kersee. They are not fat, and they have well-defined, firm muscles. Under his fur, your dog should look and feel like that. If you want your dog to be an athlete, then it is only fair that you do what you can to help him achieve the body that he will need to perform and stay healthy and injury-free for many years.

Remember that, when a dog is jumping, each pound of body weight translates to much more than that when landing. The force on landing depends on the weight of the dog and the maximum height of the dog's trajectory (not the height of the obstacle). If your dog jumps 30" and clears his jumps by at least two inches, he's falling from 32", and that's a lot of force. Now, if your canine friend is carrying an extra 10 pounds of fat (which many performance dogs are), you are assigning him that much extra weight to propel to that 32" height and much more than 10 extra pounds of force on landing for each jump. That's a lot of unnecessary wear and tear. Apply that force year after year, and you have enough cumulative wear to cause permanent damage to joints, ligaments, and tendons.

If your dog is overweight by the above criteria, now is the time to get him on a diet. There is no magic formula to determine the amount of food that a dog should eat. Weight gain or loss is determined not only by the amount of food ingested, but also by the quality and digestibility of the food, the activity level of the dog, and the dog's rate of metabolism. As in humans, the correct amount of food to give a dog is best arrived at empirically. Barring certain medical conditions such as hypothyroidism, if your dog is healthy and is overweight, he is eating too much or is not exercising enough, or both. To help your dog lose weight, reduce his total caloric intake (including treats) by ¼ to ⅓. Give him fresh green vegetables or canned pumpkin to fill him up and add roughage. And increase his exercise! Diet alone cannot make your dog strong. Once you have put your dog in great physical shape, you can feed a bit more or less according to each day's activity level. Consider using baby carrots or other vegetables for treats. Most dogs love vegetables!

How can you determine whether your dog has good muscle size and tone? Kneel behind your dog while he is standing facing away from you. Lift one hind leg up and feel the muscles of the other hind leg. The muscles should be large and firm, and you should be able to feel several different groups of muscles on the upper and lower leg (muscle definition). Repeat this process for the other three legs.

Health Assessment

The best thing that you can do for your dog's health is to become a good observer. It is the need for astute observation that differentiates human from veterinary medicine, for while you can describe the pain in your abdomen to your physician, your dog depends on you to notice the change in his stance, the decrease in his appetite, or even something as subtle as a lack of sparkle in his eyes that signals pain or illness. You are like the nurse in the Emergency Room who performs triage, deciding who needs to be seen immediately and who can wait for a while if things are busy. It is up to you to observe your dog and to decide when a visit to the veterinarian is warranted.

By observe, we mean not only the things your eyes see, but the observations of all of your senses: the dry hair coat that you touch, the scraping of a claw on the ground that you hear, the flatulence that you smell, and most of all, the sixth sense you experience — the feeling that something is not quite right with your canine friend. We encourage you to trust that sixth sense and to find a veterinarian who will give credence to your senses as well as his own.

The ability to observe is not inherent — it is trained. Begin by watching as many dogs as you can at each performance event you attend. Start by looking at the big picture. Which dogs seem to move effortlessly and which appear to struggle? Can you identify any possible reasons why? Put your hands on as many dogs as possible. Feel the differences in their shoulder layback, in their weight, and in their muscle size and tone. Observe your own dog. Have a friend work your dog while you watch, or have someone videotape you while you work your dog. Rather than looking at the things that will make or break you in competition, observe how your dog moves. Look for a wagging tail, a flowing gait, and a relaxed facial expression. Over time you will amass a large mental database of observations to draw on, and you will become astute at identifying minute changes in your dog's appearance.

What are some observations that should concern you? First, you should investigate any lack of symmetry between the right and left sides of the body. Does your dog prefer to rest his weight on one leg more than the other? Are the muscles of one rear leg larger or more firm than those of the other side? Does he wag his tail more to one side than the other? You should also be concerned if your dog's performance drops off or if he has difficulty with or refuses to perform an exercise that he willingly performed before. Always give him the benefit of the doubt. Before you blame his failure to perform on a bad attitude or try another training technique to remedy the problem, be sure that he is not trying to tell you that he hurts or does not feel well.

When you need professional help, seek out a veterinarian who has some experience with performance dogs and preferably one who has observed your dog's performance event(s) and understands its physical demands. Ideally, your veterinarian should be a good diagnostician (this primarily means he is a good observer), a good listener, should have an excellent facility with helpful staff, and should be willing to refer you to a specialist such as an orthopedic surgeon for confirmation of diagnosis and/or treatment.

A discussion of canine health is not complete without mentioning genetic disorders such as hip dysplasia. Hip dysplasia, a degenerative disorder that causes arthritis of the hips, is probably the most common condition that can affect canine performance. The incidence of hip dysplasia is highest in the larger dogs (over 40 lb.), but it does occur in smaller dogs. Because this condition is so common, we recommend that all large dogs be tested for hip dysplasia. Testing small dogs is certainly recommended if the dog shows any signs of rear leg lameness. There are two techniques (Orthopedic Foundation for Animals (OFA) and PennHip) used to diagnose hip dysplasia (See Appendix B). Both involve X-raying your dog's hips, although the radiographs are taken with the dog in different positions, and the report you receive contains different information. Regardless, the radiographs need to be taken and read by an experienced veterinarian.

Using the OFA technique, your veterinarian will send the radiographs to the Orthopedic Foundation for Animals for evaluation, and you will receive a report on your dog's hip status. Although your dog can only be certified clear of hip dysplasia if he is two years of age or older when the radiographs are taken, it is worth having radiographs taken earlier (between 6 and 12 months) and sent to the OFA for preliminary evaluation. Recent data from the OFA indicates that 94% of dogs will have the same or better rating at the age of two as they had at their preliminary evaluation. So why go through the procedure twice (at 6-12 months and again at 2 years)? There are two reasons. First, your dog will be training and perhaps even competing before the age of two. If you know that he has hip dysplasia, you can take extra care to moderate his exercise and to target his conditioning program to strengthen his rear legs and spinal muscles to compensate for the hip joints which are not functioning at peak efficiency. Second, one of the most successful surgical techniques for dogs with hip dysplasia, triple pelvic osteotomy (TPO), can only be performed if the dog has not yet developed arthritis, and arthritic changes often are evident well before the age of two years.

The PennHip technique provides a very different perspective on hip dysplasia. This technique measures laxity in the hip joint, thought to be the initial alteration that leads to hip dysplasia and arthritis. Instead of stating whether your dog is or is not dysplastic, the PennHip report compares the degree of laxity in your dog's hips to others of his breed. The principle is that if you breed your dog only if it has a better score than most others in the breed and only to an individual with a better score, you will reduce the incidence of hip dysplasia. The advantages of the PennHip system are that dogs can be tested at a younger age, and they need be tested only once. On the other hand, at least at this time, PennHip evaluations cannot be used as a basis for deciding whether to have surgical procedures such as TPO performed. In addition, the number of dogs that have been tested using this method are much fewer than by OFA, making it difficult to determine the significance of the findings, particularly in the rarer breeds. Further, there are no baseline data for mixed breeds, and currently there are only a limited number of veterinarians in the United States that perform the procedure. At present, it is our opinion that PennHip evaluations are of more value for breeders than for those interested in evaluating their performance dogs.

If you find out that your dog is dysplastic, and TPO surgery is not an option, does that rule out training and competing in your favorite performance event? Usually not. Many dysplastic dogs compete (and win) in obedience, agility, and other events that require jumping. However, dogs with hip dysplasia need to be conditioned more carefully than dogs with normal hips. They need to be given a **moderate** amount of exercise on a regular basis — no more weekend warriors! Swimming is by far the best exercise for a dysplastic dog because it improves cardiovascular fitness and joint suppleness without stressing the hips by weight-bearing. If your dog has hip dysplasia, you need to be extra sensitive for signs of fatigue or pain. Remember that if both hips are equally sore, your dog may not limp. The only sign may be a slight grimace — a tightening at the corners of the mouth. You should always be aware of the footing, and consider pulling him from training or competition if the ground is very uneven or slippery as after a heavy rain. Because his hip joints don't fit together tightly, a bad slip can cause damage to the ligaments that are holding the hip joint together, causing acute pain and accelerating the development of arthritis.

As if testing for hip dysplasia weren't enough, a number of breeds have a significant incidence of elbow dysplasia, and in these breeds, elbow radiographs should also be obtained and evaluated by the OFA. In some breeds, a cardiac and/or eye examination is also recommended. Your local or national breed club is a good source of information on genetic problems that are common in your breed. If your dog is a mixed breed, you will need to consider his parentage (if known) when deciding what conditions to check for. However, because hip dysplasia is so common, he should probably have his hips tested regardless.

Physical Conditioning

What exactly does conditioning mean? Simply stated, conditioning consists of a planned program of exercise and nutrition.

When designing an exercise program, consider the dog's age and current level of fitness, any pre-existing medical conditions or injuries, the performance event(s) the dog will enjoy, and the handler's time and physical constraints. Although young puppies can be introduced to some of the skills and tools of their future trade, conditioning exercises such as roadwork^ that stress the musculoskeletal system should not begin until well after the growth plates have closed (at approximately 10 months in small dogs and 14 months in the larger breeds). The growth plates are the locations in each bone where new bone forms, and damage to the growth plates can result in serious limb deformities.

Dogs that are overweight must be trimmed down and exercised more gently in the initial stages of the program. As with dysplastic dogs, swimming is superior exercise for overweight dogs because it is a non-weight-bearing exercise. An overweight dog also may be exercised by trotting on leash for 5 minutes every other day initially. The length of the walk should be increased gradually over a period of 8 to 12 weeks until the dog is trotting for 30 minutes at a time. At the same time, indoor and outdoor exercises should be used to improve strength and flexibility.

In all cases, an exercise program should start gradually, should be consistently applied, should provide variety, and should progress towards a specific goal. In other words, conditioning is not just a weekend activity. Some commitment should be made to exercise your dog during the week. For example, a dog that is being prepared for a national competition two months away might be taken hiking or swimming on Saturday when there is more time, and on Sunday he might undergo skill training in the morning and a 30-minute trot in the evening. During the week, when you have less time to devote to conditioning, he might be taken for a 30-minute trot on Tuesday and Thursday. On Monday and Wednesday, he might be skill trained and worked on cavaletti and conditioning jumps, and on Friday he gets to watch a movie on HBO.

There are three components of a complete conditioning program for dogs: strength training, endurance training, and skill training. Skill training consists of the goal-directed exercises such as heeling and training agility contacts that we all do to prepare our dogs for competition. But strength and endurance exercises should also be included in your program. There are two kinds of fibers in every muscle: red fibers and white fibers, also known as fast-twitch and slow-twitch fibers. These fibers differ in their rate of energy utilization so that the red (fast-twitch) fibers are able to contract when short-term strength is needed, but the white (slow-twitch) fibers take over during long periods of exercise when endurance is required. By conditioning both types of muscle fibers, dogs will be prepared when short bursts of intense effort are required and will have the ability to call on energy reserves when endurance is required.

Examples of strength training exercises for dogs include short re-trieves on land or in the water, running short distances, playing chase, and jumping. Endurance training involves repetitive activities performed over time, such as swimming or trotting long distances or pulling a sled over several miles. Every dog should be provided with skill, strength, and endur-ance exercises each week, and dogs that are actively training and competing in sporting events should be exercised more.

Because we all have trouble sticking to a program which is no fun, you should choose doggie exercises that suit you. Your program will also depend on where you live, your available hours, the number and size of the dogs in your family, your favorite canine sports, the location at which you normally train, opportunities to get outdoors, your dog's playmates, and his favorite games. The following are some of our favorite ways of exercising and conditioning our performance dogs. They are divided into two main categories: outdoor and indoor exercises.

Outdoor Exercises

Even if your dog is tiny enough to run indoors, outdoor exercise is best for conditioning because of the uneven surface. An analogy can be made to your riding a stationary bicycle or jogging on a treadmill. It's a good indoor workout, and it can strengthen some major muscle groups, but it doesn't give you the benefit of the constant minor adjustments your body must make in response to the imperfect feel of outdoor terrain. Therefore, riding a real bicycle or jogging outdoors is a far more useful conditioning exercise because, in addition to major muscle groups, these activities work many interrelated support structures, improving balance, joint stability, peripheral strength, coordination, and body awareness. Likewise, playing indoors with your dog is certainly beneficial, but not nearly as useful from a conditioning standpoint as outdoor play. So by all means, play with your dog inside, and don't throw away his treadmill, but choose outdoor exercise instead whenever you can, for body and mind's sake.

The outdoors generally affords better traction and take-off and landing surfaces for jumping as well. That, and the wide-open feeling, allow our dogs to stretch out and power their bodies. They learn a lot about sharp turns and coordination at speed, and they perfect the body awareness they will need to handle unexpected footing or tricky jump sequences. Another thing about the outdoors is that it makes us more alert. We and our dogs breathe more deeply, move more briskly, and act more like animals! It's good practice for the exciting atmosphere of a competition.

The following are five major kinds of outdoor conditioning exercises. Hopefully you can gain access to at least three of them:

1. Hiking In The Woods
This is in a class by itself — the best all-around conditioner. If your dog can run free and scamper over, under, around, and through the many natural obstacles, up and down hills, through the marsh, and over the rocks, he's developing strength in every single muscle he'll ever need for jumping, and he's also covering many times the distance that you are walking! In some terrain, the little dogs have more maneuverability than the big dogs, and in other areas, the big dogs move more easily. They work it out and are smarter and happier for doing so. Needless to say, you need to work up to full capability gradually for each dog. Your woods dog also needs a reliable recall and a collar he can slip out of in case it gets caught on a branch. We also recommend carrying a leash, just in case.

If hikes are not your thing, or you don't have access to woods or a park where dogs can run free, a walk on a retractable leash is much better than nothing. But keep going at a good clip — don't let your canine friend stop at every bush that smells inviting. Don't forego your walk because of bad weather unless you plan never to show your dog at a trial in such weather. Just dress for the elements and enjoy yourself!

2. Games

Sometimes we forget how to let ourselves play, but it's great exercise, and it's also a resource for when our dogs are feeling insecure. And playing is good exercise for us, too. How about Tag, or Find It? Kids are a great inspiration, since they always have an active game up their sleeves. If your dog loves kids, you could supervise their play together, anything from Doggie-Ball Soccer to Hide 'n' Seek. You could hire an older child to walk your dog. Give the kid and dog mutual cookie-power recall lessons first, even if they'll be on leash. It's good insurance for mishaps, and it helps the child keep control. If your dog doesn't love kids, you can still get some new game ideas by watching or asking them.

Doggie group free-for-all play is great if you trust the individuals, and no one dog gets picked on exclusively. The usual showing off behavior leads to an occasional nose-dive and accidental incivility, but it's healthy for your canine friends to deal with this unless you see something really threatening. Generally, friendly groups of manageable dogs get so much good out of these play sessions that they are worth the small risk of injury. Like any other intense exercise, though, hard play requires real strength, so don't send a couch potato into a group of seasoned roughnecks, and be a bit protective of high-energy dogs who are out of shape, for the call to action may be stronger than the dog. Gradual acclimatization with fewer and less active dogs is important, along with a general strengthening program. One game you should try to avoid is Crash Test Dummies. You know — the one where two dogs signal each other from some distance away and run full tilt into each other. This game can result in serious injury.

3. Swimming

This exercise is great for joints, flexibility, heart, and lungs. It doesn't build muscle strength or bone density or burn off the fat as well as running does (because it's not a weight-bearing exercise), but long swimming sessions are about the best way to improve cardiovascular fitness and suppleness in the body. Swimming is such superior exercise for dogs of all ages that you should promise to train your next puppy to swim. Most 7-week-old puppies are natural swimmers and can be encouraged to swim by walking with them in a creek with shallow areas that they can trot through and slightly deeper areas where they can swim to catch up. The kiddie pool or bath will also work.

You don't have to work too hard to give your dog an excellent swimming workout. A small pond and a good throwing arm are great. Julie's dogs love to follow the rowboat in their 1-acre pond, and they chase the Boomer

Ball® for miles without coming to shore. It's terrific exercise, especially for the spaniel who swims the entire session while barking at the Rottweiler who won't let him control the ball. If you don't have access to a pond, or the ponds near you are dangerous (broken glass, alligators, etc.), your dog can get excellent exercise by swimming in a pool. You can walk around the outside of the pool while the dog swims alongside you. Drop an occasional dog cookie in the water (most of them float) a little ahead of the dog to keep his interest up. Be sure to go in both directions. Swimming in this fashion helps build endurance. In contrast, short retrieves in water build strength because the dog has to push himself against the barrier of the water each time he enters and exits.

4. Roadwork

This builds muscle and bone strength and is a good choice for people who don't have the woods for hiking. Roadwork is best performed on leash to keep the dog at a steady pace. Most people can walk fast enough to keep a small-to-midsized dog trotting. For the larger dogs, it is necessary to do some power walking (3.5 to 4 mph) to keep up with your canine friend (Fig. 5-1). Even at that speed, most large dogs will be jogging rather than trotting. Jogging is good exercise but not as strenuous as maintaining an extended trot. Mountain bikes, in-line skates, horses, and cross-country skis are good human transportation to keep up with a dog at an extended trot. It is best for the handler to perform exercise of some form with the dog to maintain an aware-ness of the level of effort exerted by the dog and environmental conditions such as temperature and humidity. If you must use a car, you should have a helper drive while you take responsibility for the dog. Do you know a jogger who'd like company? A good target range is 4-8 mph for medium dogs and 6-10 mph for big dogs. Speed and distance depend on terrain, weather, and the size and condition of your dog. A 20-pound canine athlete can be roadworked by a weekend jogger, but many big dogs are too fast for that. Some can trot at 12 mph, which means 5-minute miles — serious running for a human!

Perhaps because they can ride alongside the dog, people sometimes overdo roadwork. Dogs should not begin intensive roadwork until they are fully mature, and a dog should not be roadworked two days in a row. The muscles need a chance to repair and regenerate after the intense exercise that roadwork provides. It is essential that the dog be monitored for overheating or fatigue while being roadworked. If there is one design fault of dogs, it is their inefficient heat control mechanisms. Remember, if you feel too hot, you can be sure that your dog is suffering more than you!

Figure 5-1. It is convenient to attach your dog to a waistbelt such as those used for skijoring so that your arms can swing at your sides and remain free in case of an emergency.

The minimum exercise standards set for humans are 20 minutes of sustained exercise at a time, three times per week. The latest research says that fat is burned best and strength and endurance are improved most if we work at less than the formerly recommended 80% of our maximum capability. About 65% of maximum is best. We might do well to experiment with numbers like these for our dogs as well. As a general rule, you'll get better conditioning out of roadworking at 5 mph for two miles than at 10 mph for one mile.

5. Retrieving

This is a very popular method to exercise dogs, especially for those living in the city, because it doesn't require open spaces. It also appeals to people because the human can stand still while the dog gets the exercise. However, it does have some potential for injury, particularly for dogs that scramble to capture that ball-prey before it gets away! The risk of injury can be significantly decreased by not letting the dog catch up to the thrown object until it has stopped moving. You can do this by holding the dog or telling him to stay until the ball stops, or by whacking a tennis ball with a racket so far that the dog can't catch up to it until it has stopped. Because they can change direction with the slightest gust of wind, Frisbees® as a retrieving tool should be thrown low to the ground to prevent the dog from twisting on landing. The rear legs of a dog are not built to support the dog's weight on landing, and injuries of the spine and rear legs are common in disc-catching dogs.

Indoor Exercises

When you can't get outside, there are lots of things you can do indoors to help strengthen parts of the dog's body, just by spending a few minutes a day playing games or teaching certain tricks. These are just a few of our favorites.

1. Play Bow

This stretches the muscles and ligaments of the upper body and strengthens the haunches and spine. You probably won't have to formally teach this position because canids have been play bowing spontaneously for millions of years. Just praise, name it, and reward it when you see it (a 10-second game of Chase-Me may be the best reward). When you set out to solicit a play bow from your dog, assume a similar position yourself at a time when your dog is receptive to play, and immediately offer a large reward along with praising and naming the behavior when he responds with a bow or partial bow at first.

2. Upside-down Stretch

This may look a bit weird, but it's certainly a great relaxing stretch for the spine and upper body. Obviously, dogs have to be trained to do this. It's easiest to teach it to young puppies. When your pup has just stepped out of his crate, with a good stretch foremost on his mind, rub his chest and tummy with one hand while supporting his rear end by resting the upper part of the rear legs on your arm (Fig. 5-2). As the pup grows, you can raise the rear up a little so that the dog rests more weight on his front end (and you don't have to bend as far or support the weight of the rear; Fig. 5-3). The stretch is provided by gravity, of course, so this strange-looking body stretching is far more smooth and effective a stretch than any human-handed gentle pulling of relaxed limbs and body while the dog is lying down. Because of the male anatomy, this technique can be difficult with a male dog. An alternative is to have your male dog reach up and rest his front paws on your chest. You tell him to stay and step back so that he has to rest more of his weight on you and his back curves and stretches.

3. Flexibility

Dogs who are flexible jump and turn more gracefully and they land more softly. To work on side-to-side flexibility, have your dog standing, brace his haunches against one of your legs, and invite him to wrap his body around your leg in order to reach an enticement. Don't bend his body your-self. Just invite him to take a step with the front while you support the rear to prevent swinging out. The dog decides how much bend to offer. Make sure you practice bending to both sides.

Figure 5-2. Teaching a puppy to stretch.

Most adult dogs are more flexible in one direction than the other. Your dog will show his preference during jumping, preferring to turn one way or the other on landing. Like humans, the majority of dogs are right-handed and want to turn clockwise. If you are not sure whether your dog is right or left-sided, observe which way he turns before lying down. There is also a simple exercise you can do. Draw a 20-foot straight line on the ground and sit your dog at one end of it, facing the other end. Have a friend hold your dog's favorite toy, rev him up by waving the toy around, and then place the toy at the other end of the line. Send your dog to get it, and make note of which way he turns after picking it up. He doesn't need to know how to retrieve — even little puppies enjoy the chase and will turn around when you call. Repeat this twice more, and the best two out of three will indicate whether your dog is right- or left-sided.

Figure 5-3. The upside-down stretch.

4. Catch

This simple game improves eye-mouth coordination, attention, concentration, and flexibility. Begin with popcorn or a small stuffed toy for non-
naturals; the ever-popular tennis ball is more difficult. Toss gently at first.
Many dogs who seemed to be completely incompetent with this skill have
become proficient by working with patient, encouraging teachers. The worse
your dog seems to be at this initially, the more the skill can help him become
better coordinated.

5. Crawl

This exercise can really build a strong rear, especially if you teach
your dog to crawl with his hind legs tucked underneath him rather than

stretched out behind. It also works the spine, shoulders, and neck. The easiest way to teach the crawl is to sit on the ground with your legs together, knees elevated, and entice your dog to follow a cookie under your leg (or under a coffee table for a very large dog). Be sure to give a piece of cookie for each forward increment of progress at first. Request more and more effort for each treat as your dog becomes stronger and more proficient.

6. Sit up

The world's favorite small-dog parlor trick is very beneficial to the dog's spine, balance, and rear assembly. It's easily taught by shaping the behavior, which involves rewarding the dog for each increment of improvement toward the full behavior. The first step might be to reward your dog for lifting his paw or shuffling his front feet while he's sitting. When he realizes it has something to do with moving the feet and does that repeatedly as if to train you to reward him, then you can require that the front legs be lifted higher before you reward him. The behavior of raising up both front feet at

Figure 5-4. Standing tall and still takes strength and balance.

once while sitting is indeed easier for small dogs, so it may take only a couple intermediate steps to accomplish the full behavior. Big dogs may need several intermediate steps.

The basic sit-up involves raising only the front legs. Stronger dogs are able to extend the quadriceps muscles while holding the front legs elevated, which lets them rise up on their back legs. This requires more balance and rear end strength. Dancing, or shifting weight back and forth between the back legs, is easier than standing still with back legs extended (Fig. 5-4). Standing tall and still takes more balance. Note, however, that dogs with problems such as severe hip dysplasia or arthritis in the rear legs should not be asked to perform this more difficult exercise.

Figure 5-5. The wave (suitable for use at sporting events).

7. Wave

This is a great shoulder stretch, and shoulders are vulnerable to jumping injury from the force of repeated landings. They need to be supple as well as strong; they need to flex as much as the skeleton will allow to absorb the shock of forceful landings. A straight-arm leg lift can also strengthen your dog's biceps tendon, which is equally vulnerable in jumping. Strains of this tendon are a common and sometimes career-ending injury among athletic dogs. Use a shaping process to get your dog to lift his whole arm high, without flexing the pastern. Remember, the first step of a shaping process may look nothing like the finished product! Your dog may be bending his pastern in Step 1, but eventually you will be able to shape that away as he tries to lift his leg higher (Fig. 5-5). Then you'll reward only straight-leg lifts.

Another variation on this exercise is to have the dog wave while sitting up. The sit-up exercise strengthens the spinal muscles which are responsible for bending and straightening, while the wave strengthens the muscles that are responsible for side-to-side movement.

8. Tug

Though this game has a mixed reputation, it's a wonderful spine-flexing, overall strengthening exercise. Just be sure to teach the dog to release the object, even if tug is played only between dogs at your house. It's quite useful, both for training and for competition, to teach your dog a tension-relieving game like tugging on the leash. You might want to set a ground rule that he plays tug by invitation only if you don't want him to insist on playing it whenever he likes. Some people worry that retrievers and other hunting dogs will lose their soft mouth if encouraged to play tug, but we have not found this to be the case.

9. Back up

This is another of those little-used but versatile exercises. It builds strength and suppleness through the spine and hindquarters and also improves coordination and body awareness. It's easy to teach this exercise using a handful of tidbits. Walk gently into your dog's chest, and give a cookie immediately when your dog steps backward (or hops backward while sitting). When he begins to take over the job before you nudge, you can reward that initiative and wean from the body-touching. As with any shaping process, the first step looks nothing like the finished behavior. Ask for more effort from your dog only when he's ready to give it.

One of our favorite and most exerting indoor exercises for medium and large dogs is a very advanced version of backing up using stairs. To teach backing up the stairs, begin at the top of the stairs and use a fistful of cookies to entice your dog to walk his front feet down the first step only. Give him a cookie for this, since it is a strange request. The cookie and your body keep him from continuing down the stairs, provided that he really is strong enough to anchor himself with his quadriceps. This is only for very strong dogs who already understand the command to back up! When you first ask your dog in this position to back up, he may not be able to figure it out, in which case just use one hand under his belly and the other on his chest to assist him while praising him, and give him a cookie at the top. He'll take over the job as the coordination of it becomes clear to him. As your dog gets stronger and more experienced, he can learn to back up multiple stairs. This exercise is not for the marginally fit; it stresses every single body part.

Mental Conditioning

To be successful in competition, mental conditioning is essential. The best way to condition a dog mentally is to provide frequent periods of play and to incorporate play into the skill training exercises. Play is an essential part of a dog's emotional make-up. Games such as Tug-of-War and Chase-the-Owner used to be considered harmful but are now understood to be a way to relieve the dog's stress through play, while at the same time increasing his focus on the owner and strengthening the dog-human bond. In addition to frequent play breaks, be careful not to overtrain, whether it be in conditioning or in skill training. Keep a journal of your dog's training activities and refer to it frequently, making adjustments in the frequency, duration, and intensity of training sessions in order to provide variety and prevent staleness. And remember — just like you, every dog needs time off!

In addition to your dog's mental conditioning, it is essential that you work on your own stress level. Learn to recognize the warning signs — the physical and emotional clues that you are beginning to lose your patience during training or are unable to concentrate on your teamwork with your dog during competition. There are a number of books that provide valuable suggestions for getting the human half of the team under control.

Getting your dog in shape for athletics shows respect for him, and it will also give you and your dog a new dimension of enjoyment together. A fit dog is an amazing athlete; one that can have a long and happy career.

6. Jumping For Obedience

We have devoted one chapter each to the subjects of jumping for obedience, agility, and flyball because each of these sports has different rules and contexts for jumping. This requires that dogs competing in each of these sports be trained to cope with the individual complexities of the sport. Of course a dog can compete successfully in all three sports — the training methods provided are not mutually exclusive, but rather are complimentary.

It is not our purpose to present every detail of how to train your dog to perform each component of the obedience jumping exercises. These training techniques are well presented by many different trainers and are detailed in training books. Instead, the purpose of this Chapter is to help you gain a perspective on how your dog views obedience jumping, to give you an idea of the issues that make obedience jumping unique and sometimes difficult, and to provide you with techniques that will help you make obedience jumping safer and more fun for your dog.

In comparison to agility competition, in which the handler never knows the obstacle course until the day of competition, obedience jumping, with its strict rules regarding the appearance of jumps, the location of the jumps within the confines of a measured ring, the consistent nature of the jumping exercises, and the order in which they are executed, may seem very easy. But looks can be deceiving. There are a number of elements that make obedience jumping difficult enough to be a challenge to many dogs. These challenges and suggested ways to cope with them are listed below.

The Challenges of Obedience Jumping

Solid Jumps

Whether your dog is competing at AKC, UKC, or CKC^ jump heights, the solid jump is literally a blind leap of faith. The AKC jump heights, which are 1¼ times the dog's height at the withers, prevent the dog from seeing the landing area on the other side of the solid jump. Unless your dog resembles a giraffe, even the UKC and CKC jump heights, which are equal to the dog's height at the withers, make it difficult for the dog to see where the dumbbell lands and impossible to see the ground where he will land. These jumps, therefore, require that the dog have an extra measure of confidence, both in his ability to land on unknown footing and in your not putting him in an untenable position. It is your responsibility to train him to be a confident jumper and to ensure the safety of this blind jump.

The First Jump Phenomenon

In obedience, all of the jumps are first jumps. There are never a few jumps on which to warm up or with which to test the footing. The dog is always jumping cold. It is rare in any athletic endeavor that one's first try at something is his best. There are several ways you can help your dog to get a better first jump during competition. They include giving your dog enough room to accelerate sufficiently before the jump, training him to bound right into a canter from your side, and training him to select the correct trajectory for his size and conformation and for the size of the ring.

Limited Ring Size

The AKC rules require that outdoor obedience rings be a minimum of 40 feet by 50 feet, and they permit indoor rings to be smaller: 30 feet by 40 feet is acceptable for an indoor ring for the Open class, and 35 feet by 50 feet is required for an indoor Utility ring. These rules are meant to be beneficial to the host clubs, which may have trouble finding a spacious indoor venue. But they inadvertently penalize the dogs. Indoor rings can rarely provide adequate footing and padding for soft landings, nor do they provide sufficient room for the larger dogs to achieve the speed necessary to jump with a flatter trajectory.

Fronts^

As if it were not enough that the larger dogs have limited space in the obedience ring, for four jumps out of five, the dog is required to decelerate rapidly after jumping and place himself in a sit, straight in front of the handler (within a couple of inches of straight is not good enough for full marks). For the fifth jump, the dog has to decelerate rapidly to pick up a dumbbell, execute a 180 degree turn, and speed up again to repeat the jump. These rapid changes in speed require that the obedience dog be in tip-top physical condition and have excellent control over the movements of his legs and spine. These can be achieved through good foundation training and by keeping your dog fit.

Turns After Jumping

All jumps in obedience, with the exception of the return trip over the high jump in Open, require that the dog turn soon after landing. In the case of the broad jump and the first time over the high jump, the dog must turn a full 180 degrees. It is logical, therefore, that dogs that are being trained to jump for obedience should receive deliberate training in how to turn before and after jumps. But how often does that happen? For a variety of reasons — lack of equipment, lack of space, or lack of knowledge or originality on the part of the instructor, the majority of obedience training classes teach jumping by rote. They place the dog in front of the jump and call the dog over, or run by the jump with the dog, or throw something for the dog to fetch after jumping, and then at some point, they ask the dog to turn and come back over the jump, frequently with the jump at almost full height.

Call-backs, as outlined in Chapter 3, teach the dog to be comfortable turning 180 degrees after jumping, and from there you need just to put the call-back into the context of the obedience exercises, first as a separate exercise, and then as a part of the final picture. From the beginning, you should not give the call-back command until the dog has landed and taken at least one complete stride straight ahead. This will help pattern the dog to move forward a bit before turning and will lessen the chance of the dog turning in the air and either cutting the corner of the broad jump or landing with his body partly turned, which places stress on the legs and spine. To help your dog move straight ahead after landing, throw a toy so that it lands well beyond the center of the jump. Begin to delay the throw so that the dog has to commit to the jump before seeing where the toy will land. Then you can wean the dog from the toy by throwing it intermittently or by occasionally hiding it out there prior to his jumping.

Footing

Depending on the climate, obedience trials may be held indoors or outdoors, and thus may offer a variety of different types of footing. Outdoor trials generally provide the best footing, although if held on thick, spongy grass, the jumps may remain elevated on the blades of grass while the dog's feet sink in on take-off, thus elevating the effective jump height by an inch or two. This emphasizes the importance of training using a variety of jump heights and providing foundation training that includes experience with different types of footing.

Indoor shows are a bigger problem. Most of the time the footing consists of a single layer of rubber or vinyl matting over concrete. This unyielding surface significantly increases the impact on the dog's front end when landing from a jump, especially when the dog is using a rounder trajectory (Fig. 6-1). This puts the larger dogs in double jeopardy, because not only do they hit the ground with more force because of their weight, they have to jump with a rounder trajectory because of the limited ring size. The best indoor footing consists of matting laid on rubberized flooring as can be found in some gymnasiums. Even mats on wooden flooring are more forgiving than concrete.

Figure 6-1. Most indoor venues with matting on concrete result in greater concussion on landing than outdoor sites.

Beware of vinyl matting. It tends to be stiffer than rubber matting, and therefore more difficult to keep flat. In addition, on humid days in a cool, non-air-conditioned building, condensation can form on vinyl matting, making it extremely slick. At outdoor shows, be careful when it is raining or when there is a lot of dew on the grass in the early morning. The ground outside the ring may provide good footing, but the areas where dogs have been taking off and landing can be very slippery. It is your responsibility to ensure that the footing is within your dog's comfort level. If you arrive at a show and discover that the footing is not safe, you should mention your concerns to the host club. If it appears that there is no remedy for the situation, you should excuse yourself from competition. Your teammate is trusting you to make that decision for him. If you tell him to, he will jump.

If your dog has a physical problem that affects his jumping, such as hip dysplasia or arthritis of the shoulders, give serious consideration to limiting your competitions to outdoor shows. Or at least limit the number of indoor shows at which you compete — just go to the ones that you know have the best footing. And let the host club know how much you appreciate their safer venue.

The Bar

Have you ever been forced as a little child to sit in church for what seemed like hours? You might have found yourself staring at a row of pillars along the church wall, and as you stared, they seemed to move in and out and turn strange colors. Well, sometime you should sit and stare for a few seconds at the bar jump bar at eye level about 8 feet away. You will see the black and white stripes change places with each other and seem to move in and out past each other. It's an obstacle illusion. Kids' science books are full of other such examples. Perhaps the bar was originally designed that way in the assumption that it would be more visible to the dog. But it is important for the handler to be aware of how difficult it can be for dogs to recognize exactly where that bar is in space, especially if there is another repeating pattern in the background, such as a row of small trees. Be sure to include one or two black and white striped jump bars as ground poles in your early training lanes and continue to use them when you shift over to jumps. This will give your dog lots of practice judging how far away they are.

The Dumbbell

Do you have trouble walking and chewing gum? Well, some dogs have trouble jumping and holding a dumbbell. The most common reason is ill-fitting dumbbells — usually ones that are too large and thus slip from side to side in the mouth. Sometimes dumbbells can actually block a dog's vision;

this is particularly true in the toy and brachycephalic dogs (with shortened muzzles, such as Pugs and Pekinese). In these breed, the bells of the dumbbell may be very close to the eyes. The solution is to first ensure that your dog's dumbbell fits snugly and that the bells are of a size and shape that don't interfere with vision (Fig. 6-2). Second, spend some time teaching the dog to jump with an object in his mouth. Practice first on poles on the ground and allow your dog to develop confidence with fancy footwork while carrying an

Photo by Jim Comunale

Figure 6-2. The bright-eyed bounce of this dog tells us that the dumbbell is no problem.

object. It doesn't always have to be a dumbbell — why not use his favorite stuffed toy too? Include lots of play to make it fun. Play tug-of-war with that stuffed toy to convince him to hang onto it tight. And then do some more training.

Training Obedience Jumping

If you haven't done so already, you should train your canine companion through at least the first two levels of the Complete Jump Training Program outlined in Chapter 3. This will provide him with a solid foundation in the ways his body moves and in the principles of jumping. If your dog has any jumping problems or shows a lack of confidence, even occasionally, it is well worth the time to build that foundation now. Jumping is one of the few things in life that becomes progressively easier and more fun once the basics are fully mastered.

Having mastered Levels I and II of the Complete Jump Training Program, your dog will be familiar with bar jumps, broad jumps, and solid jumps. (This is the reverse of the way that dogs are often introduced to the obedience jumps — frequently they never see a bar jump until they already have a CDX.) A refresher on the use of the solid jump can be given by adding a solid jump as one of the jumps in a jump circle, with the jumps set no higher than elbow height. The jump circle is used because it lets the dog see at least some of what is on the other side of the jump. After the dog is confident with the solid jump as part of a circle, you can then add it to other patterns as described in Chapter 3. You can increase the height of the solid jump to chest level while performing these patterns, but when it is time to build up to competition heights, the solid jump should be jumped only as a single jump. High solid jumps are not appropriate in complex sequences because the dog cannot see past the jump, and therefore does not have sufficient time to make in-air modifications or on-ground adjustments.

Once your teammate is familiar with all of the obedience jumps, you can start to teach him formal obedience jumping exercises. As the best trainers will tell you, the first step is to break each exercise down into its smallest component parts, and train each of these separately. The following are some aspects of jump training unique to obedience that you should be aware of when training.

Holding an Object While Jumping
You have already shown your dog that it is fun to carry a toy around in his mouth while traversing ground poles, and he will gladly hold the dumbbell in his mouth. Now you can put that correctly fitting dumbbell into his mouth and have a friend hold him in a sit 15-20 feet away from the jump which is set at elbow height. Cross over to the other side of the jump and call him. He doesn't go around the jump, because with all of the fun jumping experiences he has had, he loves jumping! When he gets to you, praise him! No fronts, please! Leave those until both his jumping and his fronts are absolutely solid. After he has jumped the solid jump in one direction, have him jump it in the other direction. This is especially important in the early stages of training so that he will learn to picture the jump from both sides. Be sure and train him to jump with the dumbbell in his mouth at each new height.

Choosing the Correct Trajectory
For most dogs, the correct trajectory is different for each of the obedience jumps. If your dog is small (40 lbs. or less), there will usually be enough room for him to choose a flat trajectory. For the larger dogs, the appropriate trajectory for the solid and bar jumps in the obedience ring is usually a more

rounded trajectory. Your dog can still choose a safer, flat trajectory for the broad jump, and that will reduce his chances of turning in the air.

How do you help your dog choose the safest trajectory? This begins with the jump training program outlined in Chapter 3, which teaches the dog to be a thinking, confident jumper and to be able to select an appropriate trajectory for the available space, footing, height of the jump, and how energetic he feels that day. You also will have determined his first jump set-up distance (see Chapter 3, Level III). The following are a number of additional guidelines to help you.

Remember to leave enough room for your dog to take at least two, and preferably three (and for small dogs, there is room for four or more), strides before his take-off spot. The more room you give him, the better he will be able to accelerate, and the flatter will be his trajectory. As an extra bonus, by giving him lots of room, you will help him to collect himself after the return jump and thus increase the chances of getting a straight front. There is nothing magical about setting the dog up two strides in front of the jump. If there is room for three, make it so!

Second, during the early stages of high jump training, before you have taught him to return over the jump, teach him a high jump command that is separate from the retrieve command and his other jump commands. This command will mean, "Charge towards the jump as hard as you can!" Then, when you begin to train the return, give him that command as soon as he picks up the dumbbell. Don't leave him out there in space. So often we are taught to set the dog up carefully, exactly two strides ahead of the jump. But then we throw the dumbbell to the other side of the jump, and leave him to pick up the dumbbell and figure out the best way to return. How unfair!

In the Utility Directed Jumping exercise, your dog has to judge the correct take-off point by himself (the jumps may be different distances away, depending on how straight his go-outs were), determine how flat a trajectory he can afford while not running into the ring barrier upon landing, and execute a turn of approximately 90 degrees. This requires substantial foundation training with jumps that are a variety of distances apart from each other, at different distances away from the dog, and at different angles to the dog's path. This exercise is one in which the dog utilizes the hip-swivel to turn the rear legs so that they will be ready to propel him toward you upon landing.

Turning Safely After the Broad Jump

Several things have already been mentioned that will auger for a safer turn after the broad jump, including training for a flatter trajectory, using a toy as a target when training the broad jump, and giving the dog enough room to accelerate and decelerate. One more thing should be added. Make it a rule that you never call your dog to you as soon as he lands. Let him take a stride or two before you ask him to turn. Put up a barrier that prevents him from turning too soon. With repetition, this will become habit.

Working Up to Full Height

The key to getting your dog up to competition height is to do it slowly. There really is no rush. There is no glory at all in having the youngest dog in your class in a trial. Further, just because he jumps a given height several times in one training session, or during several training sessions in a row, or for a given number of days or weeks, does not mean that he won't benefit from further training at that jump height, or even from dropping back to a lower height occasionally. Why not add some other components to increase the difficulty and provide your dog with more experience at that jump height? Have him approach the jump at an angle, provide distractions, add the retrieve, and take him to different locations so that he can experience different types of footing. Increase the height gradually, 1-2 inches at a time (make a 1 inch high jump board) until you reach his regulation height. Then train him to jump a little higher, for insurance.

Even after you have worked up to full height, don't train exclusively at that height. In fact, you should train at full height less than half the time. Vary the heights often, even several times in one training session. All he needs is an occasional reminder of full height. When you train indoors, lower the heights substantially unless you have access to a facility with ⅜" or more of underpadding under the mats.

Learning to Throw the Dumbbell

The location at which the dumbbell lands can make or break your Retrieve Over the High Jump exercise. It is important that you get a dumbbell that is designed and constructed to bounce as little as possible. We have found that although plastic dumbbells last longer (especially if you have a chewer) and work as well as wooden dumbbells outdoors on grass, the wooden ones absorb the shock of landing on the harder indoor surfaces much better and therefore tend to bounce less. It doesn't matter what technique you use to throw the dumbbell, but it does matter that the dumbbell lands in a location that permits your dog to make the return jump as safely as possible.

What are your dog's needs for the return over the high jump? This varies depending on the dog's size and favorite jumping style, but the following are some basic necessities. First, your dog should be centered on the jump after having picked up the dumbbell and turned. That means that unless your dog can turn on a dime or turns prior to picking up the dumbbell, you shouldn't throw the dumbbell so that it lands opposite the center of the jump. If your dog is right-sided (prefers to turn to the right) and picks up the dumbbell before turning, as most dogs do, then the dumbbell should land slightly to the left of the center of the jump (Fig. 6-3). If your dog is left-sided, then the reverse is true. The amount by which the dumbbell is placed off-center depends on the size of your dog and how tightly he turns. Be warned — if you have a right-sided dog and throw the dumbbell too far to the left, he may have to turn to the left to pick up the dumbbell and will probably continue to turn to the left afterward, putting him way off course for the return (Fig. 6-4). By helping your dog end up centered on the jump for the return, you not only help him to jump more safely, but you also increase the chances of getting a straight front after he lands. This same principle can be used, by the way, to help you get a straight front after the retrieve on the flat.

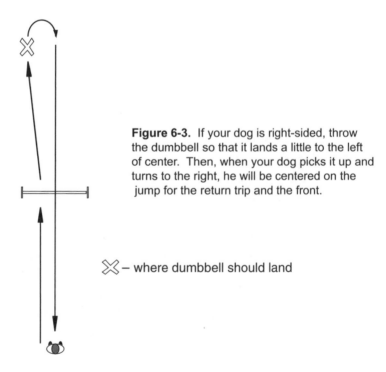

Figure 6-3. If your dog is right-sided, throw the dumbbell so that it lands a little to the left of center. Then, when your dog picks it up and turns to the right, he will be centered on the jump for the return trip and the front.

✕ – where dumbbell should land

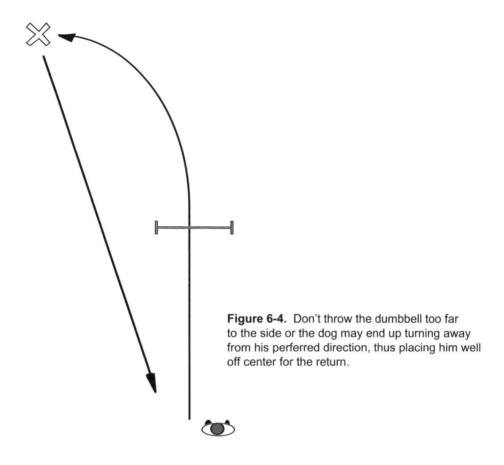

Figure 6-4. Don't throw the dumbbell too far to the side or the dog may end up turning away from his perferred direction, thus placing him well off center for the return.

     Having established at what point opposite the jump your dumbbell should land, you now need to decide how far from the jump it needs to land to give your dog room to accelerate and arrive at his preferred take-off spot for the return jump. The main thing to remember at this point is that your dog is standing, not sitting, after picking up the dumbbell, so he will more than likely trot for a few steps before shifting into a canter for jumping. That means that the dumbbell should land further away from the jump than the distance at which you set him to begin the exercise. Just how much further away depends on your dog's size and how quickly he accelerates after picking up the dumbbell. This distance is best arrived at by trial and error. Once you have determined that distance, practice throwing the dumbbell to the correct location many times, on many different surfaces. For fun, if you like to compete against yourself, draw several concentric circles around the spot on the ground that you have determined would constitute a perfect throw, and score yourself to see how close you get. This is one way of being sure that you improve.

The nice thing about this exercise is that this is one part of obedience that is totally up to you — the dog plays no part in the landing of the dumbbell, so you are in control!

One last (but **not** least) piece of advice: remember to keep it fun! Obedience, with all of its required precision, is much more stressful than would appear by the amount of physical activity your dog has to undertake. Remember to break off for play often. The best time to do this is when you feel like it the least. If you feel yourself getting tense because your dog is making mistakes, stop what you are doing. It would be better to do nothing than to continue. But better still would be to control your frustration, think of what a good friend your teammate is, remember that the competition ahead is a very small matter in comparison to your lifelong relationship, and start to play with him.

7. JUMPING FOR AGILITY

There is no dog sport that calls for more jumping or more wits while jumping than agility. This sport is a myriad of obstacles, testing your dog's ability to go over, under, around, and through all manner of equipment with speed and accuracy. The order of obstacles and flow of the course are not known ahead of time, so agility cannot be rote-trained. It requires concepts, not rituals, so it favors a smart jumper.

Jumping is a major component of all agility classes, and the upper level international-style jumpers classes are particularly demanding. The combination of difficult jumps, variable spacing, and hard turns requires superior strength and a clear mind.

And some dogs just make it look so easy, don't they? Jumping is as natural to them as breathing. Why not just get one of them? Well, that's one option, of course, and it's exactly what many agility competitors decide to do, at least the next dog around. But that isn't the only good option, and we're here to prove it.

You can help your average agility dog become a good jumper by using the Jump Training Program described in Chapter 3. Your dog may have a hidden talent for jumping that just needs guidance to bring it out. Or you may have a dog who will work at his skills with you and become that wonderful combination of ability and accountability that so many talented but helter-skelter agility dogs have yet to find.

The very top agility dogs are power jumpers; they have the talent to stretch out and soar over jumps where the course is roomy, but collect themselves and jump with tucked hindquarters where the course is tight and tricky. This allows them to make very fast time where they can, but execute tight turns and avoid traps where they need to be more conservative. In the horse world, they would be called complimentary things like "scopey^," which refers to their superior athletic ability. It's an informal assessment of the overall structure and attitude of the individual, a meshing of physical and mental talent.

A power jumper develops a good eye for the terrain and a good mind for choosing the best take-off spot. His body moves like it can handle anything. On an agility course, he can see the opportunity for speed or the necessity for caution based on the handler's activity and the placement of upcoming obstacles. So even where the jumps are all approximately the same height, he does not take off the same distance away from each jump. Where he sees an open jump sequence, he takes off earlier, at greater speed, thereby covering more ground during his time in the air. When the dog has his mind on handler instructions or tight turns, he covers less ground at a slower speed. The dog can turn in the air more easily on a rounded trajectory with his haunches tucked underneath him. To do this, he swivels his hips without having to counteract the centrifugal force of trailing legs.

If you have a natural jumper, hopefully you have used Chapter 3 to develop your dog's accuracy and honesty along with his experience. A talented dog who is trained quick and dirty usually ends up cheating by the time he's running agility courses. Many an average but honest jumper has walked away with the prize over dozens of more talented jumpers who didn't have a clean run that day. Performance standards continue to rise, and some-day all the winning runs will be breathtaking, but not until the very talented dogs improve their percentage of clean runs.

With this chapter, you can add more vocabulary to your dog's considerable repertoire, including "around," "pass," "get out" and "come in," "left," and "right." There are also some sequences to help you practice changes of side and to increase your dog's ability to turn in the air. (For dogs who already have some agility jumping problems, such as repeatedly knocking bars, see also Chapter 9). But more important than all the words and exercises in the world is your dog's ability to read your body language, and your ability to read his, while running two different paths and negotiating obstacles at two to five yards per second. That kind of skill is based on teamwork.

There's a simple formula for teamwork: Teamwork = TLC (Trust, Leadership, Confidence). The book *Enjoying Dog Agility* devotes Chapter 4 to this view of teamwork and how to build it. To oversimplify just one element, trust must be earned, not demanded. Once it's in place, don't take your dog's trust for granted. The more timid dogs need to trust you in order to give new challenges a try. See to it that they view every attempt as a success. The more independent dogs need to trust you in order to take your advice. See that they are rewarded for listening.

A general instruction like that may seem simple, even obvious, but it's anything but easy. Should you really reward your timid dog for a pitiful attempt? Yes! What is more, you should reward your timid dog for showing initiative, even toward the wrong obstacle. This builds teamwork faster than telling him he's wrong and redirecting him. To be sure, you need to redirect him, but you also need to compliment what, for him, was a brave decision to approach an element of difficulty, perhaps distance work or jumping a spread, even though you didn't ask.

And for the independent dog who needs to be rewarded for listening in order to foster his teamwork? He deserves to be rewarded for calling off his intended plan, even if he guesses wrong about exactly where to break off and come toward you, or knocks the jump down in trying to turn at your request. It's important that you understand just what is difficult for your dog and what elements of teamwork you need to reward especially. Those elements are worth reinforcing. If you wait for everything to be correct at once, you are missing many opportunities to reinforce important elements and making it difficult for your dog to know exactly what you liked when you do reward him.

Learning is complicated and does not happen smoothly for any of us. It's a jigsaw puzzle which cannot be pieced together all at once. We have to try various pieces in various places until they fit. Agility jumping is some of the most complicated jumping your dog will ever perform. There are so many elements of difficulty and teamwork involved that you must develop a feel for rewarding what you do like at the instant you see it in order to help put that one necessary piece of the puzzle in place. Once that piece is in place, you can stop being so excited about it (though you should never take behavior completely for granted). You will never run out of pieces to reinforce in agility jumping because the puzzle is so big and complicated. Just when you think you've got it all together, a piece you thought was firmly in place begins to loosen. That's what behavior does. A trainer should expect this.

When you first see an uncharacteristic but desirable quality begin to emerge in your canine teammate, it is likely that it will be somewhat out of place. If you can encourage that thinking on your dog's part when you get the opportunity, even though it was not part of your lesson plan at that moment, you will be fostering long-term teamwork. There is time later to reward the same response only when you ask for it, and that's a necessary step, but first you need to recognize and greet it when you're lucky enough to get it. Your dog is trying to stretch his thinking in the right direction, and agility jumping requires a thinking canine. Your selective reactions to your dog's unsolicited behaviors will cumulatively determine the growth or repression of beautiful teamwork. Good training is a two-way street.

As you build on the background provided in Chapter 3 and take your jumping skills even further for agility, bring your patience and ingenuity along. The finished teamwork that produces smooth, clean, seemingly effortless runs time after time requires a lot of experience. Experience provides the opportunity to learn from our mistakes. It's up to us whether we make each mistake a constructive learning experience. If we let the same mistakes keep happening to us, we will end up with some very well-learned mistakes. Agility is full of these, especially missed contact zones and bad jumping habits. Though the average dog can earn basic agility titles without extra jumping skills, the advanced classes call for more skill. Here are some hints for bettering your agility jumping and communication beyond the basics.

Additional Commands For Agility Jumping

Around
With so many advanced courses calling for awkward approach angles, it's helpful to be able to send your dog around to a better approach without having to stop him. A signal, perhaps a scooping flick of the wrist with the left or right hand indicating an arc to the left or right, is also useful. Note: If you use the word "around" as an obedience command, obviously you need to choose a different word here, and pay special attention to your dog's tendency to stop at heel position. That means you need to reinforce especially the step past heel position if that is a snag for your dog.

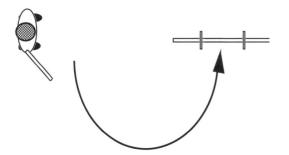

Figure 7-1. To begin to teach "around," position yourself end-on to the jump and send him away from you to one side or the other and over the jump.

The easiest way to help the dog conceptualize this is by leading him around your body with a cookie, perhaps while sitting backwards on a chair to prevent him from misunderstanding. Pass the cookie behind your back (some dogs need a tidbit when you change hands). Wean from the lure by having the dog go further and further around you before getting the food, until he takes over the job and knows how to train you to give him the cookie by running around you on command. Signal with your non-cookie hand. Now teach the other direction the same way; don't expect an automatic transfer of direction. All in all, it takes several steps to shape this understanding, but that foundation will transfer the skill to obstacles quite easily.

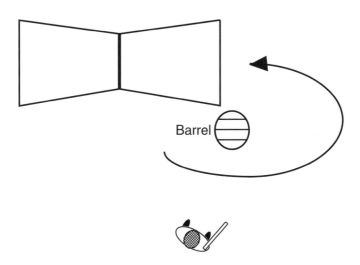

Barrel

Figure 7-2. You can transfer "around" to contact obstacles by providing an object such as a barrel for the dog to go around, thus giving a better approach for the contact obstacle.

Choose an object, such as a barrel, that you can reach around at first, in case you have to entice him with a cookie a couple times. Once he will go around that in either direction according to your signal, bring the skill quickly to other objects, like cars, tables, and rooms in your house.

Now you're ready for jumps, and here you will really appreciate this skill. Begin with a low jump, and position yourself and your dog end-on to the jump, so he can't know which way to take it (Fig. 7-1). Give your command and signal to send him away from you and over the jump. Help him the first time (lure/leash), so he won't think you want him to circle the jump. He'll learn quickly that you're giving him an approach command.

This skill will transfer well to contact obstacles. You will be able to save time by sending your dog around to the end rather than interrupting him or risking his hopping on from the side. This is easily taught by using your barrel or a traffic cone as a context cue for the command with gradually increasing approach angles (Fig. 7-2). Wean from the cone by changing its position and by reviewing easy angles without the prop.

Pass

This means, "Don't take that obstacle!" A resilient dog can be taught this on the agility course, preferably on leash. Just walk him up to the jump, say, "Pass" and immediately turn him away from the jump and reward him. Many dogs tend to over-generalize this, as if you were telling them not to jump anymore. It's a good rule of thumb, therefore, to teach inhibiting things away from the sport first, and then bring the learned skill to the sport. "Pass" can be taught outside of the context of agility using cookies or toys. Hold up a cookie and say, "Okay", then give it to your dog. Then hold up a cookie and say, "Pass." If your dog moves to take the cookie, close your hand on it and discourage him appropriately. For some dogs you may simply need to say, "No, pass," while for others, a bop on the nose may be necessary to back them off the cookie. Only when they can come forward with confidence for the cookie on "okay" and resist the cookie without stress on "pass" are they ready to bring this skill to the agility course. Now do the exercise with the jump as described above, and your dog will remain confident.

Come in; Get out

These handy directionals mean "come toward me" or "go away." Get out is often accompanied by a full-arm signal to specify exactly where to go, sometimes called "pushing the dog out." This work makes you appreciate a dog's superior hearing, sensitivity to motion, and peripheral vision (about 120 degrees, as opposed to about 90 degrees for a human). Dogs can note the signal even when working in front of you, seemingly not noticing you.

"Come in" is readily taught on leash, keeping in mind that the leash is for reinforcing control, not for punishing mistakes (Fig. 7-3). The leash prevents a wrong choice by making the right choice clear from the outset because your dog is well-trained to follow the leash and keep it slack. The leash should not be your choice if you expect to have to jerk it. In that case, you need to work on the informal attention exercise from Chapter 3, Level II. It is assumed now that your dog loves his leash and that it relaxes him about making choices and the complexity of the work.

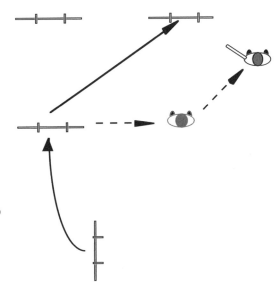

Figure 7-3. Teach "come in" by using body language to encourage your dog to choose the correct jump.

"Get out" is taught as an extension of a send-away (see Chapter 4), or as a wider "around," by placing two jumps next to each other and insisting on the further jump with an exaggerated, pushing arm signal and a forward step into the path of the closer jump while focusing on the further jump (Fig. 7-4). Make sure to place the two jumps very close to each other at first, so you are not sending your dog far enough to confuse him. Introduce this on leash for very sensitive dogs, or teach it separate from agility obstacles entirely, using two barrels to extend your "around" command. Eventually, "around" refers to a nearby obstacle and "get out" sends your dog further away. It's quite useful for your dog to know both directives.

Left; Right

These words are not for everyone. Don't use them if you get mixed up under pressure, especially when your dog is facing a different direction from you. Remember that his line of travel will not always be perpendicular to the jump he is taking, so the obstacle that looked straight ahead in the walk-through may actually be a left or right to him when running the course at speed. It's particularly difficult to use directional names with dogs who tend to look away from their line of travel. Naturally, it's the direction from your dog's perspective that counts, not yours.

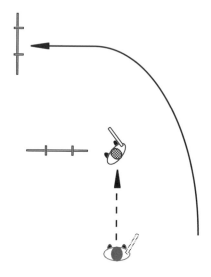

Figure 7-4. "Get out" is taught by placing two jumps close to each other and insisting on the further jump with an exaggerated, pushing arm signal and forward step into the path of the closer jump.

The vast majority of dogs who appear to be going by direction names are in fact going by body language and voice location. Very few dogs have actually been thoroughly taught to discriminate between these names, mostly because the handlers have been too quick to mistake coincidence for learning. The dog does have a 50/50 chance of guessing correctly, and going by body and voice location offers a near-perfect system. Julie gave a 'left and right' demo at one seminar and had everyone clamoring to learn how she taught direction names; then she explained that this dog didn't know those names. His perfect responses were really based on more subtle cues.

For those who can keep the directions straight in the context of agility, there are a few times when directional names really can save the day. To teach them, one foolproof approach is to teach one direction at a time. It's helpful to begin by using the signal exercise from Chapter 4 and substituting the directional name for the signal. The dog is not really guessing at first, of course, since the reward is calling him to the correct side. But it helps him move his body in response to the word without your having to move your body. This is a critical element in a conceptual understanding of the word. A good next step is to send your dog away through a short straight tunnel and call the direction while he's inside. Reward only turns in the correct direction on exit. Ignore wrong turns. Dogs who like to chase toys can be told which direction the toy will be thrown just prior to its release. Don't throw the toy if the dog heads the wrong way, or you'll create a frantic dog who charges either way and looks for the toy to signal a change of direction. That's counterproductive.

By the way, you can't ignore behavior by scowling, laughing, or criticizing the dog, but only by looking straight ahead for a few seconds, watching the dog only with peripheral vision and not moving your body. Five seconds is plenty, then invite him to try again. The contrast of your excitement and attention when he guesses correctly is quite a reward, which you might also supplement with a special treat.

Once you have the basic response, you will be ready to vary the variables, and that will certainly include substituting a low jump for the tunnel, adding a jump on exit from the tunnel, using multiple jumps, etc. There are many potential variables, and they all need to be played with. Just don't introduce more than one change at a time if you want to bring your dog along smoothly. So that your dog will be comfortable turning in both directions, you may want to teach your dog's less flexible direction first.

When the dog will cheerfully turn in the correct direction during a short sequence a few times in a row without a big reward, and before introducing too many complicated variables to the first direction, interrupt the first direction work to teach the second direction concept. The second direction goes slowly at first, but then gains conceptualization rapidly. It's important to start over at Step 1, because there will be some resistance to the change. That's how well you taught the first direction. Working through a manageable level of frustration is an important element in concept learning, and it's also a good way to improve the mental stamina your dog will need for advanced agility work.

Additional Body Language For Agility Jumping

Top-level agility is intricate teamwork, a dance of balance. Imagine a fast-paced number where each partner has his dance space and responsibilities, but the choreography is *ad lib*. Body language and timing become all-important, and the partners must read each other effortlessly.

Your dog begins learning to read you from the moment you meet. He may be quite expert at it now, but agility calls for some additional fine-tuning. These games will help your dog learn to focus on your body cues. Eventually, he'll need to be able to read you when he's working in front of you at speed, and, what is more, he'll have to remember to do so even when he's excited and when he thinks he knows the course already.

Crossing Behind Or In Front Of Your Dog

Someone has to have the right of way on a complex course, and generally it's the dog. The handler is captain, navigator, and chief strategist, but the dog needs a clear path from one obstacle to the next. When a change of side is required, you will need to cross either in front of or behind your dog. There are advantages to each strategy; neither is right or wrong.

Crossing in front requires that you get across the right of way before your dog needs it. Your dog must continue on course in spite of your sudden movement ahead of him, and you must learn the timing required to cross without interrupting his present obstacle or impeding his speed or flow. Crossing in front is much easier when your dog is working at less than the speed of light. The big advantage is that you enter the next tricky sequence with your dog already knowing which way he will be turning next. The disadvantage is that you must be fully in position and ready earlier than when you cross behind.

Crossing behind your dog requires that you commit your dog to the correct obstacle ahead and allow him to pass before you dart across the right of way behind him. Your dog must maintain his commitment to the obstacle in spite of your sudden movement behind him. You must be patient enough not to cut your dog off, and you must leave yourself enough maneuvering room to cross without crowding your dog from behind. In other words, a good job of crossing behind requires send-away skill. The big advantage is that your movement to one side or the other behind your dog cues him as to direction, and you have an extra second, sometimes two (plenty of time!) to get fully in position to indicate the next obstacle.

The 4-jump sequences in Figure 7-5 can help you experiment with crossing behind and in front. In each case, assume that the handler (dotted line) starts beside the dog and ends up beside the last jump. More advanced teams may require less movement and less advanced teams more, but this is useful for comparison, showing a two-point handling strategy for each choice.

Does your preferred strategy change when the sequence looks like a pinwheel (Fig. 7-6)? How and why? What about four parallel jumps?

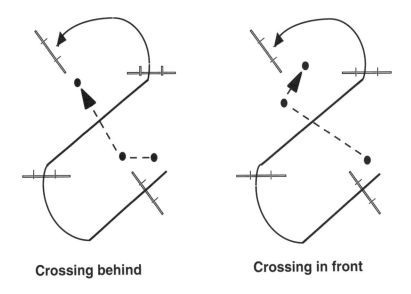

Crossing behind   **Crossing in front**

Figure 7-5. 4-jump sequences to practice crossing behind and in front of the dog.

Many handlers take the opportunity to cross while the dog is in a tunnel or jumping a loop of jumps. The handler gets into position to direct an upcoming tricky spot from the other side.

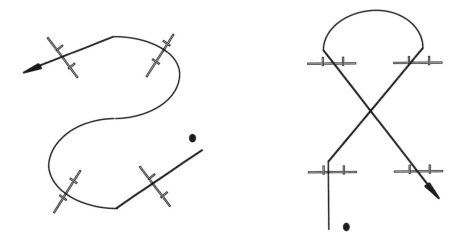

● = handler's starting position

Figure 7-6. Practice crossing in front of and behind your dog with the pinwheel and parallel jump configurations shown here.

Better Turns While Jumping

Turning in the air saves a great deal of time by saving distance; the dog who is turning in the air is headed the correct way on landing rather than making wider arcs than necessary from one jump to the next. More efficient turns also make it easier to stay on course; the wider the arc, the greater the likelihood of taking a wrong obstacle en route.

Here is where very flexible dogs have such an advantage. But all the flexibility in the world won't save the run if the dog isn't paying attention to his handler. The key to practicing good turns in the air is to begin where the dog can be successful. On leash is ideal. The handler's job early on is to give the command in plenty of time for the dog to cooperate without stressing his body or his mind. The call-offs and call-backs described in Chapter 3, Level II are prerequisite to these exercises, and the flexibility exercises outlined in Chapter 5 may be important for your dog.

The **jumping square** is a well-known tool for teaching directional sensitivity. Instead of introducing the square at full jump height, use it extensively at lower heights (vary the heights), and gradually bring the sides in quite close to mimic the quick timing you'll need to perform tricky control sequences at course heights and course distances. Figure 7-7 provides a few routines for helping your dog learn to bend in the air. You can think of many more!

Which is your dog's more flexible side? Practice quick spins for cookies to his other side. If your dog tends to turn to his more flexible side rather than bend efficiently to the correct side, the leash and cookies are your basic friends. You can also help by stepping early and wide toward the

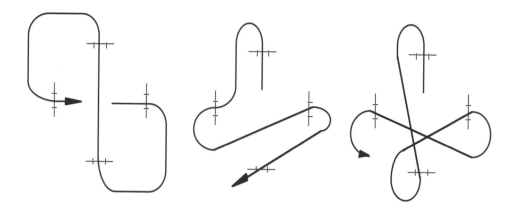

Figure 7-7. Sample jumping square configurations for teaching directional sensitivity.

desired side to entice your dog's attention toward that side. Make sure to praise at the instant your dog anticipates correctly! It's his decision to turn that way at that instant (which you should praise, not merely the completion of the entire exercise). Enjoy the learning process.

One important caution: it's not fair to go into the jumping square or any of these patterns without a plan for your own body movements, signals, etc. See Chapter 3, Level II, Step 4.

Take 2, Skip 1

This is another useful and simple configuration (Fig. 7-8) which, like the square, allows you to work on or off leash with jumps at any height and distance. Simply start your dog as if he were going to jump all the jumps in the circle, but call him off after jump 2. Skip jump 3, and send him out to do jump 4. It makes no difference which obstacle is jump 1. The basic sequence is this order: 1, 2, skip 3; 4, 1, skip 2; 3, 4, skip 1.

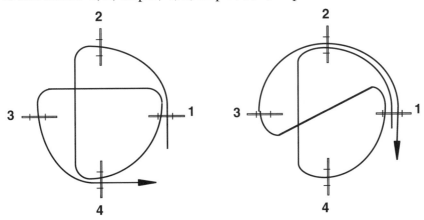

Figure 7-8. Take 2, skip 1 configurations will help you to consolidate the "around," "pass," "come in," and "get out" exercises and to practice crossing behind and in front of your dog.

As with other training setups, many variations are possible. Try this: 1, 2, skip 3; 4, 1, skip 2; turn as you greet your dog in the middle and send to jump 3 from the other direction, then do jumps 3, 2, and 1. This pattern is drawn on the right above.

Remember, plan each run, stick to it so as to give clear body language, and use whatever enticements you need to help you and your dog get it right. These exercises are only to get you started. Think of these and all your other bright ideas for body language lessons as *teamwork* exercises. The exercises are successful each time you and your dog understand each other's body language. You're not trying to dance alone.

Video

As your agility career takes shape, and you and your dog are working on full courses, you'll become increasingly interested in handling strategy, teamwork, and the details of what goes wrong from time to time. Your best training tool now may be a video camera, especially for studying jumping. Watching your work on tape is the best way to learn what really happened out there. And, to recognize the fine points of handling and jumping, like timing, body talk, take-off spots, trajectories, clearances, in-air modifications, and details of style, you'll need to study dogs and handlers in slow motion and even frame by frame. It's enough to drive any normal household crazy, but it's incredibly useful to the hard-core enthusiast.

When studying your agility run this way, try to put yourself mentally back on the course so you can remember what crossed your mind at the instant in question. What did you see on the dog's face or in his stride at that moment? What were you feeling? How did those thoughts help or hinder your work at that time? Can you see a dance of balance between you and your dog? What were your shoulders, arms, and face telling your dog? How can you improve skills in yourself and your dog? Don't forget to get past any frustrations or jubilations and on to the business at hand — learning something constructive from the experience. Once you've done that, you can start planning for improvement, which is a continual process. You and your dog are on track for long-term teamwork and personal growth.

8. Jumping For Flyball

The flashy sport of flyball made its appearance on the dog sport scene in the 1980s, shortly before agility. With guidance from the North American Flyball Association, which was established in 1984, the sport evolved by leaps and bounds. The equipment is fairly simple, consisting mainly of four jumps and a box, the trigger-happy contraption that dispenses tennis balls directly to the mouths of impatient canine racers.

Years of aggressive redesigning revolutionized the flyball box from a tin can on a spring-loaded throwing arm to its current amazing rapid-fire efficiency (so efficient that a controversy arose when spectators could no longer even see the ball being delivered to the dog). Original spring-arm boxes are still seen occasionally, and new boxes are always being designed. As with other athletic dog sports like obedience and agility, distinct interpretations of the sport have sprung up, so there are less competitive, more spectator-oriented competitions, as well as the cutting edge of keen power and speed records.

Flyball is a relay race, with four dogs on a team. In turn, each dog charges over four jumps to the box, operates the box appropriately to release the tennis ball, and returns with the ball over the same four jumps. The jumping factor in flyball has remained unchanged from the beginning. This includes the four jumps themselves, always white in color and 24" wide, with 10' spacing from one to the next, the first jump positioned 6' from the start line, and the last jump positioned 15' from the box. With a jump height range of 8" minimum to 16" maximum, the official jump height for a flyball team is 4" lower than the height of the shortest dog on the team.

Two parameters for flyball jumping skills are readily distinguishable from the complicated jumping seen in international-style agility. First, flyball jumping is not as demanding in terms of jump height. The height of the jumps, per se, is not meant to be a limiting factor for participation. Second, the entire setup: the appearance of the jumps, their spacing, and their height, is the same from one competition to the next, so the performance of the jumps can be trained as a ritual. Concepts are important for the single-minded pursuit of tennis balls that might get away and for other variables which could occur during a meet, but the jumping parameters for flyball are set in stone. How convenient! We can have a lot of fun with that.

The following three sections can be worked in any order or combination. They give hints for teaching the three major elements of difficulty associated with flyball jumping: speed, the bounce, and the return. Although it would seem that flyball is a simple and carefree game and therefore a great sport to start with youngsters, young puppies should not be doing this! Their appropriate level of jump work is described in Chapter 3, Level I and in Chapter 4. They can be building skills and attitudes that will help them greatly in flyball, but this program is too strenuous for the immature pup.

Speed

The top flyball teams nowadays are inching the speeds down by hundredths of a second, hovering around 17 seconds for a four-dog team. Four seconds per dog, down and back! The modern flyball box is so efficient (allowing dogs to grab and turn with the ball in about a second) that the speed of the dogs is the deciding factor. Teams in the record-breaking league are running over the jumps at about 11 yards per second. A quick glance to line themselves up and one stride to get into position, and they are in a dead run on automatic pilot over the jumps. Because of the low height and the mandated spacing between jumps, we can teach our dogs to stretch out and jump flat for flyball.

Jumping flat describes the body of the dog, which is horizontal over the jumps with front legs reaching forward, head and neck stretched forward, and hind legs stretched back (Fig. 8-1). The back is flat rather than rounded. Jumping flat also refers to the trajectory or the dog's arc over the jump from take-off to landing.

Photo by Tom Schaefges

Figure 8-1. This flyball dog uses a flat trajectory to speed over jumps.

You can help your dog become an efficient flyball jumper. Being foundation trainers, we recommend you first go through Chapter 3, Level I, for your dog's general jumping education. It will improve his body awareness and his ability to restart himself when he runs into difficulty.

After that, start with simple jumps. There is no need for jumps higher than 6 inches yet, and certainly 3 inches is plenty for small dogs. The lower the jumps, the easier it is for your dog to bounce rather than stride between them. If your dog is very small (or inhibited with his body), start with jumps spaced 2½ feet apart. If he's mid-sized, start at 5 feet apart. A really fast small dog may belong in the 5 feet group. Very hard-driving larger dogs might even be comfortable immediately at 10-foot spacing, but it would be wiser to start them with jumps about 7½ to 8 feet apart, because to begin with 10-foot spacing invites the dog to take extra strides. You'll get to 10-foot spacing quickly, and you'll get there with better flyball jumping habits if you gradually lengthen your dog's running stride rather than set him up early on to take an extra stride.

Make your series short at first, perhaps 4 to 6 jumps (about 10 to 15 feet in total length for small dogs and 20 to 30 feet for large dogs). Trot your dog over the jumps on leash, on both left and right sides (he will have to become fully comfortable in flyball with commotion going on either side of him while he's running, so working with you on both sides is just the first step of gaining that comfort level).

As soon as your dog likes this game, work off-leash, and then begin calling him over the jumps as described in Chapter 3, Level I, Step 4. Use your favorite tricks to keep him fast and eager.

Bounce

When a dog jumps one jump and then another with no stride in between, it's called bouncing. It's very quick. When jumps in a series are unevenly spaced, such as in agility, a bounce between jumps can make the next jump more challenging by crowding the dog at an odd stride away at full speed. The dog must lengthen and collect on the run to adjust quickly to the odd striding between jumps. But the flyball system of 10-foot spacing between each jump in the series makes bouncing the most efficient way to get down the line. The dogs just have to learn to take off and land about five feet before and after each jump. That can be taught gradually, beginning with the dog's own natural bounce stride and teaching him to lengthen (or occasionally to shorten) that stride to 10 feet when he plays flyball. Bouncing the flyball jumps can be accomplished by most medium and large dogs. Small dogs need to find a flat-out striding rhythm. It will come automatically with speed as long as you work gradually, since a dog trying to go his fastest lengthens his strides to the maximum (see Fig. 2-9).

As your dog becomes adept at traversing the jumps, the most important variables to change are the total distance run (work up to over 50 feet) and the distance between jumps. Initially you can remove every other jump for the small dogs, bringing them up to five feet between jumps. The medium dogs can move up to 7½ feet. If your dog adds extra strides, work up more gradually.

Note: These increments generally work well, being comfortable and logical fractions of the 10-foot goal. But they are only guidelines, and you should be ready to experiment for your dog if he seems uncomfortable with any spacing. It is not possible to gauge your dog's stride by anything less than watching your dog run. Even then, he may initially stride differently over jumps than on the flat. Many things affect the spacing at which your dog will bounce jumps. Read Chapter 3, Level III, Steps 1-4 for more on this subject.

Use of a take-off pole can help your dog learn to take off earlier rather than fit in an extra stride. Your take-off pole can be a jump pole laid on the ground in front of the jump, close enough for the dog to decide to jump it in the same stride as the jump rather than step between the two. The take-off pole shows the dog the power of taking off sooner and soaring over longer distances in the air. Gradually move it further away from the jump to encourage the dog to take off sooner and sooner. The take-off pole then should be used intermittently, since you will need to wean from it completely. It serves to introduce the dog to a different, freer jumping option, one which is much more efficient for flyball. Don't forget to praise your dog as he is soaring over your special jumps. He needs to know that you approve of his brilliant decision to jump longer distances. Praising him only at completion of the line of jumps just says, "I'm glad you got here."

Some other variables you will want to change now include raising the jump heights, your own position (from a recall, to the sidelines, to the start), working indoors and outdoors, and gradually introducing all manner of distractions on both sides. Don't teach the flyball box and the jumps in the same session. Teach all the elements of difficulty associated with the box separately, and don't bring the box and the jumping skills together until both have been learned separately. When you do start to put them together, use one jump, then two, etc.

Your dog will progress in his own way, and you will make training decisions continually as to jump heights, distances, take-off poles or not, distractions, varying the variables, when to value effort as highly as achievement, when to add additional elements of difficulty, etc. Whether your dog requires four increments of increase or ten, your ultimate goal is getting the dog fast, happy, and automatic with the jumps 10 feet apart, and as few strides between them as possible.

Return

Teaching flyball jumping with an emphasis on recalls over the jumps offers the advantage of making the return over the jumps the most familiar part of the game. It's very important that your dog always love this part! Don't take it for granted. You want to develop a dog who brings the ball back over the jumps as quickly as he goes out over the jumps to get the ball.

With this in mind, remember to add each element of difficulty to the return job in a way that your dog enjoys. Leash corrections for dropping the ball while jumping are counterproductive. Jumping while holding a ball is not so easy and should not be added to a string of jumps in one step. Teach that skill separately, and bring it well-learned to your jumping lane. Likewise, the operation of the box is a complicated series of behaviors to be taught separately. It is not helpful to criticize your dog's mistakes when you start chaining these jobs together.

A strong foundation lends itself to good jumping, and any emerging carelessness can be nipped in the bud by ignoring poor jumps and reinforcing good ones (see also Chapter 9). As with other jump training, the learning process is a critical period for timing your praise to congratulate extra effort in your dog's weaker areas. This will help him progress toward the pinnacle of the sport without losing the sheer carefree joy of this fast and happy game.

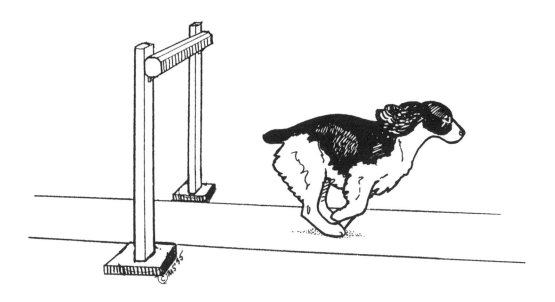

9. JUMPING PROBLEMS

If only it would not be necessary to bring up the subject of jumping problems! As every canine sports enthusiast knows, jumping problems can be very frustrating. They pop up at the worst times (such as when you are preparing for regional competition), they usually require a long-term commitment to solve, and even then, they still recur at selected times (such as when you are preparing for national competition). Why do jumping problems develop, and why do they always seem to resurface at the most inopportune times? The answer to both of these questions is the same. Jumping problems almost always arise out of a lack of confidence on the part of the dog, and because of that, they often recur at times when the dog is under more pressure to perform.

But there is good news! If you make it your goal to develop a confident jumper, and if you consciously strive to build self-esteem and a positive attitude in your canine teammate, it is much less likely that you will have to deal with significant jumping problems. The program described in this book does just that. From the time your little puppy comes home with you, you will begin providing him with a growing list of positive experiences, including exposure to different kinds of footing such as cement, gravel, grass, sand, wood chips, and forest detritus. You will encourage him to discover where his back feet are and how his front feet move in conjunction with them by helping him to trot over a variety of poles of different shapes and sizes, placed at a variety of distances apart and at different angles to each other. You will teach him to adjust his stride length, stretching it out, or shortening it as necessary to take off in just the right spot to clear the jump easily and with as flat a trajectory as the circumstances call for. As he grows, you will encourage him to experiment with a variety of jumping styles: to stretch his rear legs out fully or tuck them up, depending on his speed and choice of trajectory, to raise his head confidently or lay it down on the front legs in intense concentration, depending on the circumstances. You will help him learn to swivel his hips and use his tail as a counterbalance in preparation for a turn after the jump and to understand commands to turn this way or that. You will have helped him become less one-sided, so that he will be confident turning both to the right and to the left.

Then, when you do start to raise the jump heights, he will have all of those tools to draw on. He will know that jumps are sometimes placed at odd distances apart, or that there may not be a lot of room as in the obedience ring, and he will confidently pace himself ahead of the jump so that he arrives at just the right take-off spot. He will not be surprised by a change in footing at his take-off spot where the ground may be slippery from use. And, he will be experienced in looking ahead at the whole picture, to prepare himself for jumps that are set in a variety of combinations.

Surprisingly, it is uncommon for jumping problems to be a direct result of poor structure, although poor structure can contribute to physical problems that affect jumping. In fact, some of the most athletic breeds, like Border Collies, Belgian Sheepdogs, and Shelties have the most jumping problems. Why would a well-built, athletic dog develop jumping problems? Often it is just that athleticism that fools us. We start by asking the dog to jump a low jump. Of course he can easily clear the jump — he has jumped logs in the woods that were more challenging! So we raise the jump height, and he clears that height easily, too. Why, this is no different than pouncing on a canine buddy in play! We raise the height again, and if the dog clears that jump, we raise it again and again. We are now utilizing the Peter Principle for dogs — raise the jump until he reaches his level of incompetence. At some point, which may be early in jump training or months or even years after he has reached competition height, something happens that makes the dog lose his confidence. Maybe one day he misjudges the footing and slips and hits the jump. Perhaps he miscalculates his speed and the distance to the jump and lands on top of the jump. In any case, he now looks at the jumps differently.

He cannot remember anymore just exactly how he cleared it in the first place. He attempts the jump again, because we ask him to, and he would do just about anything for us. But he feels clumsy and unsure, and his lack of confidence builds.

You have probably had the same experience. As a child, you were playing on a trampoline, or doing cartwheels, or learning to dive. Everything went fine in the early stages, and you felt exhilarated as your body twisted and turned and you flew through the air. But then, something went wrong, and the next time you tried to perform that series of motions, you were hesitant, even clumsy, perhaps unable even to attempt the activity. At that time, your coach or physical education teacher might have identified the problem and told you what to do to solve it. Perhaps she told you to raise your arms at a certain point, which would shift your center of gravity and thus give your body that extra boost it needed to flip around.

But dogs don't explain their problems to us fully, nor have they studied canine anatomy. (Or if they have, they have us all fooled!) More important, when our dogs have a jumping problem, we may be at a loss to identify the exact problem in the jumping process. In the past, when this happened, people did the best they knew how, which usually involved lowering the jumps and having the dog repeat the jumping sequence as often as possible, then raising the jumps once the dog was able to perform at a lower height. Sometimes this worked. Frequently it was only a temporary fix because the dog did not have a well-rounded foundation in the basic body movements involved in jumping.

That is why this book spends so much time on the basics of jumping and concentrates on developing confidence and attitude before altitude. Dogs that have a solid jumping foundation will be more familiar with their bodies and with the range of motions that their bodies undergo, and therefore will have less chance of developing jumping problems. And, if jumping problems do develop, they will have enough inner strength to attempt some of the solutions that we can offer them, and they will return to their confident jumping style more readily.

Evaluating Jumping Problems

How can you tell that your dog is having a jumping problem? Once the problem has fully developed, it is easily recognized as stutter-stepping before the jump, hesitation before jumping, popping over the jump from close up, crashing into the jumps, or hitting the jump on the way over. But it is much better to try to identify the seeds of a jumping problem before it has progressed to the point where the dog is obviously having difficulty. The earliest signs of a jumping problem might include evidence of stress when beginning the jumping exercise (panting, lips pulled back, yawning, ears laid back), an increase in speed over the jump (you may mistake it for appropriate speed, but a worried dog may speed up because of a desire to get the jump over with), slowing down on the approach to the jump, ticking the top of the jump, or a change in the dog's trajectory (either flattening the trajectory by taking off too early or rounding the trajectory by taking off too late). If you identify any of these warning signs in your dog, be sure to address them right away. There is little to be gained by hoping that the problem will go away, and working on the problem right away will significantly increase your chances of curing it completely.

Once you have recognized that your dog is not jumping freely and confidently, you must first determine whether there is a physical reason for the jumping problem. This can be quite a challenge, and you may have to use all of your senses, including that sixth sense, intuition, to differentiate between physical problems and confidence problems. This is made even more difficult by the fact that physical problems can make a dog lose confidence, so the two can co-exist.

The best tool to help you determine whether your dog's jumping problem is physical in nature is a veterinarian who understands the canine athlete, and preferably one who has participated in or at least observed your sport. Such a being can be quite difficult to find, so you may need to give some guidance to your less experienced vet. First, you should give your dog a lameness examination. The best way to do this is to observe the dog from the side and then from the front and rear while he is moving at a moderate trot. If a dog experiences pain or stiffness when using a limb, he will put less weight on that leg. The result for a front leg lameness is that the head is elevated when the sore leg is on the ground and lowered when the good leg is bearing the dog's weight. The effect is the same in the rear, except that rather than looking at the head, you should observe the pelvis and note whether it tilts more to one side than to the other when the dog is gaiting. It will tilt down more when the dog is bearing weight on the good leg. Another way you can check for lameness is to stand to one side and observe the length of stride of the dog's legs. A lame leg will usually have a shortened stride length.

Once you have identified that the dog is lame, you should put your hands on both the affected leg and the opposite leg and compare the size and texture of the muscles, bones, and joints of both legs. Even if you were unable to identify one leg as being lame (perhaps you just sensed a change in

150

the way he moves), you may be able to feel an enlarged area in one leg (this may represent swelling or scar tissue) or a smaller muscle on one side (this means that the dog has been favoring that leg). This is information that you can provide to your veterinarian. No one is as familiar as you are with your dog's appearance and the feel of his body. Be persistent in trying to obtain a diagnosis if your dog has a physical problem. Ask to be referred to an ortho-pedic specialist if your own veterinarian cannot find anything wrong and you are sure there is a physical problem. It is not fair to ask your dog to jump unless you are sure that he is healthy.

Obedience Jumping Problems

It has been our observation that there are many more dogs with jump-ing problems in obedience competition than in agility or flyball. This is particularly true for dogs that have been trained exclusively in obedience, with little or no experience in agility or flyball. At first we thought this was because jumping is such a major component of agility and flyball that people don't try to compete with dogs that are having jumping problems. We thought that perhaps with obedience, since jumping is a component of only a few exercises, more people may try to compete with a dog that has a jumping problem. But after observing thousands of dogs in all three of these sports, we have concluded that there are reasons specific to the sport of obedience that cause, or at least perpetuate, jumping problems. Some of them are listed below.

Ring Size

The obedience ring is small for most dogs, in the sense that it does not allow the dog to stretch out and use himself fully when jumping. It has a confining, controlling influence on how a dog uses his body. The larger the dog, the greater this effect. A constant diet of control can be permanently inhibiting so that a dog can lose his feel for jumping freely. That is why we stress the Complete Jump Training Program described in Chapter 3. Even though the exercises superficially resemble agility more than obedience, they provide the dog with a complete program to hone all of his physical abilities and give him the tools so that he can down-modulate his activities to the confines of the obedience ring when necessary.

Solid Jump

The use of the solid jump in obedience presents two difficulties. First, the dog is unable to see the ground on which he will land, and must trust that you will not ask him to jump in an unsafe area. That kind of trust comes hard for some dogs, and their confidence can be shaken by one or two incidents in which something unexpected happens, such as the footing being unexpectedly slippery on the other side of the jump. Second, if a dog already has a jumping problem, not being able to see to the other side of the jump can exacerbate the lack of confidence that usually accompanies jumping problems.

Footing

For much of the United States and Canada, because of cold or unpredictable weather in the winter and hot weather in the summer, a majority of shows are held indoors. The vast majority of these shows have rings consisting of rubber or vinyl matting on concrete. This creates a fairly hard landing for even the fittest dogs with the best front limb conformation. A dog with a straight front (and many, many dogs have less-than-ideal fronts) experiences greater concussion on landing, and this can create a hesitance to jump because of the anticipation of discomfort. Further, because of the confines of the obedience ring, large dogs have to use a rounder trajectory in their jumps, and this results in greater concussion on landing than the use of a flatter trajectory. Dogs that are campaigned (shown for many shows a year) on this kind of footing frequently develop chronic arthritis of the shoulders (and sometimes the elbows). Dogs that live with chronic arthritis may not limp because the pain is always there to some degree, and they learn to live with it. However, chronic arthritis can contribute to the development of jumping problems.

First Jump Phenomenon

Dogs always use a slightly different jumping style on the first jump in a series. As mentioned previously, all of the jumps in obedience are first jumps because the dog has to start from a stationary position before the jump. This means that obedience dogs need to be especially savvy about how to use their bodies. They need to accelerate rapidly to ensure that they clear the jump, yet not move so fast that they reach the ring barriers. However, because the jumping component of obedience trials is relatively small and superficially seems to be less challenging than jumping for other performance events, trainers frequently fail to give dogs the foundation they need for long-term obedience jumping. This, too, can result in lost confidence and can contribute to jumping problems.

Common Jumping Problems

If you and your dog have come to accept bad jumping habits, it's time to challenge them now. Most jumping problems can be overcome.

Please study the progression of the exercises in all Levels of Chapter 3 so you'll understand our thinking about what builds on what and when to teach which skill. For example, we believe in overtraining, but we think that it's a mistake to introduce overtraining until your dog is highly accomplished (Level III, Step 6). Many jumping problems are the result of well-meaning but premature introduction of skills that the dog is not yet ready to assimilate.

In a skill as complex as jumping, there are countless potential problems. Every dog meets a pitfall someday due to a misstep, a handler's miscue, or a misinterpretation of the jump. It's how that mistake affects the dog and the handler that determines whether it remains a fluke, becomes a pattern, or digs a big hole in the dog's jumping psyche. Naturally, being foundation trainers, we feel that a solid and well-built foundation lends itself to more ability and fewer mistakes later on. More important, we feel that a foundation built slowly, full of confidence and fun, provides a nurturing cushion upon which to land when your dog does experience a setback later.

Your early investment in your dog's jumping foundation is like money in the bank. The regular dividends are nice, but the investment really pays off by covering the debt when an emergency comes up. The stronger your foundation, the more cushion you have laid for your dog so that even a nasty problem can't wipe you out.

All of the following six types of jumping problems can be helped by going back to Chapter 3, so we'll just say that once. Usually you can pinpoint the ABC element which can be of most use to your dog in solving this problem; more often than not, the answer lies in Level I. That's where jumping confidence begins.

The other general piece of advice we offer is that many dogs are having jumping problems as a result of pain, and forcing them to continue to jump is damaging to them. These dogs have big hearts; you wouldn't jump for them if the roles were reversed. As we've said elsewhere, don't be quick to dismiss a physical cause as the source of the problem — anything from a vision problem to dysplasia of the hips or elbows, from a thorn in an ear to a jammed toe, from a hormonal imbalance to a gimpy tendon. Sharpen your observational skills and stay tuned. Groom your dog's body regularly and get to know it. Palpate for soreness, burrs, and lumps. Become the expert on your dog's body as well as his mind. Problems don't arise without a reason. In the following section, we'll discuss some common jumping problems and offer some solutions.

Knocking Bars

A pattern of not clearing jumps can develop for many reasons. It is much easier to help if you can see just what is going wrong during the jumping process, so we strongly recommend that you obtain a video of several examples of your dog's jumping problem. You will gain a lot of insight by studying him on video in slow motion, especially if he is jumping across the field of vision. Jumping toward and away from the camera provides useful supplemental information. At the very least, a good video will let you learn to praise your dog at the instant he clears his trouble spot in future jump training sessions. At its best, the video will help you isolate specific skills that your dog needs to improve. You might also see some action on your own part that is contributing to his jumping problem.

The first thing to do is analyze the details. Does your dog knock only first jumps, or spread jumps, or single bar jumps? Is he taking off too soon, his trajectory descending through the bars? Is he taking off too late, so he is hitting the bars on the way up? Is he jumping too low? Does he drop a hind leg too early? What is his jumping style: does he tuck his legs tight, stretch them, or dangle them? You need specifics. You can't directly demand intangibles like judgment, carefulness, or confidence. The success of your solution is in the details.

A long-term solution always requires that you look at the dog's foundation, which undoubtedly has some holes in it. The best thing is to stop working at more advanced jumping while you retrain. But, since life isn't perfect, it is possible to embark on a long-term fix and additionally employ some quick-fix tricks. Good quick-fix tricks consist of singling out an element of correct performance that you want your dog to emphasize. Choose one simple thing that benefits this dog, something that will improve his chances of jumping cleanly. For example, let's say your dog likes to jump with his rear in a relaxed tuck position (see Chapter 2), but he knocks bars because he tends to dangle his legs too loosely. You could study how low he generally hangs his legs, watch for any minor improvement, and praise him immediately each time he happens to tuck a bit tighter.

As you can imagine, the task of watching for accidental minor improvement is time-consuming and difficult, so things will move along more quickly if you set up **focus sessions** — short, specific training sessions which will let you selectively reinforce a specific behavior of your choice. The session helps you set up and reward the improvement repeatedly, thereby building up some positive reinforcement in that particular bank account and increasing the likelihood that your dog will, in our example, tuck his back legs more tightly in the future. You could pick any one behavior to reinforce. Here is one possible focus session, based on our example.

If you want your dog to pick up his feet quicker or higher, you can help him think about that with a simple game. Straddle a jump which is about elbow height and place your dog right up snug to the jump — no room for speed. Entice your dog to jump over the jump for a cookie, then back again. This exercise lets your dog find the strength in his haunches and learn how quickly he can tuck his feet up and out of the way. Depending on the dog, you should reward initial attempts even if he doesn't jump cleanly (just to get his initiative going), and up the ante as you go. Then gradually vary jump heights, set-back distance, number of repetitions before getting a cookie, etc. This would also be a good exercise for a dog who tends to take off too early, since it precludes that and helps him get smooth and snappy with his "up and over." It might also help a dog who tends to jump too low. This would be a poor choice, though, for a dog that tends to pop jumps or stutter-step; it would exacerbate those problems. So it is important that you do your own home-work rather than just borrow other people's exercises.

You'll do your best training if you can become intimate with your dog's quirks in jumping and plan your sessions to focus on his specific needs. You may have to ignore a few other behaviors you like and don't like in order to concentrate on the one that you want your dog to think about during the session. Make each session short, concentrated, and fun. Different sessions can focus on different elements for improvement.

Your chosen focus might be quite specific. To follow the reasoning with another common example: if your dog occasionally knocks a bar by dropping a hind leg too soon, and not always the same leg, you might study on video whether he is turning in air (perhaps bending towards you) when that happens, and whether it's the inside foot which dips (it probably is). If so, you might want to practice a few jumps in an arc or circle (Chapter 3, Level I, Step 4). The tightness of the circle allows you to adjust and exaggerate the degree of bend with lower jumps. You could also use the straddle jump exercise described above if your dog tends to bend sharply toward you while he's jumping, and progress later to jumps in a circle. Your aim would be to notice and praise the tight tucking of the inside hind leg (the leg closest to you, regardless of which side of you he is on). When the leg is loose, ignore it; when it's a bit tighter, reward immediately.

There is never just one good exercise. The more ways you can attack a problem, the better. Does your dog need to be stronger? Dogs who tend to jump too low often lack adequate strength or stamina. Have some extracur-ricular fun with conditioning (see Chapter 5). If your dog tends to displace first jumps, see Chapter 6, mix in some half-stride work from Chapter 3, Level III, and experiment on your own with various low heights and claustrophobic set-back distances. If he has a problem with a certain type of jump, be sure to set up a scaled-down version in a doorway at home, so he goes over it many times a day (because attitude comes first). You might then set up several of these scary jumps in a generously spaced jumping lane. Vary all those variables from Level I, and later add other types of jumps to the lane. Use only encouragement and rewards, of course. This is no place for criticism. Be sure to reinforce the jumping of each of the feared jumps. In that case, you are praising initiative toward the feared object. Do you praise your dog if he knocks the feared jump? Yes, at first. You raise your performance standards as your dog progresses. This gradually improves his personal average on that task. (Please remember that focus sessions are only quick-fix tricks, temporary patches. You need to go back to foundation work for your long-term solution.)

Congratulating exactly the element you wish to reinforce as soon as it occurs is pivotal to the success of your quick-fix tricks. The more obscure the element of performance you want to emphasize, the better your timing needs to be. Dog trainers have long been known for their creative punishments and their precise timing of punishments. Because timing errors with positive reinforcers do not generally damage the dogs too badly, we have become much less expert in our timing with praise as a teaching tool. We are generally sloppy with it, tending to be late and to drag out the praise. This is okay when you're reinforcing a recall; you may have a window of several seconds in which any sort of praise is useful. But when the behavior to be reinforced is very brief, as it will be in most of your jumping focus sessions, you'll need a one-syllable praise word.

Imagine that you've noticed your dog knocks jump bars because he's dropping a hind foot too early. In your focus sessions, it will be critical that you reinforce just when the hind feet clear the bar, and do so consistently many, many times over many short sessions. It is much more common to knock bars with the back feet than with the front. If you've ever praised your dog for clearing a jump and then had the bar fall, this may be your problem!

If you can't praise crisply and effectively in a focus session, where your dog needs the information concisely, then consider the use of a bridging tool, such as a clicker, for training. That's exactly what it is for; it bridges the gap between correct behavior and the reward for that behavior. Briefly, the clicker is introduced to the dog by clicking it, then immediately giving your dog a treat, at least 20 times, while varying other variables (location, distractions, etc.). Then a familiar command is given, and the instant the dog complies, he hears the clicker, then gets a treat. Variables in this phase also include other familiar commands. Then you can start demanding two repetitions for one click, two clicks for one treat, etc. Once your dog knows that the clicker means "Great!" and that a reward will follow, you are ready to use it for your focus training. This is only one oversimplified aspect of reinforcement training. If you try this approach and find it makes you a more effective trainer, there is much information available to take your skills further! A modern slogan in teaching schoolchildren applies equally well to positive reinforcement for dogs: "Catch them doing something right!"

Crashing Jumps

It's always frightening to see a dog, especially your own dog, slam into a jump as if he wanted to go through it or land on top of it (Fig. 9-1). Unlike simply displacing a jump bar, crashing a jump indicates a gross misjudgment. The dog's preferred take-off spot (PTS) for the jump was actually outside of his comfort zone, or perhaps the crash was just a misjudgment on take-off (slipping on wet grass, for example). It is bound to happen to your dog at some point, and it's a nasty accident. Immediate encouragement is required. Unfortunately, some dogs seem to accept crashing as an ordinary part of jumping, and that's unnecessary. It's time to intervene and reeducate them before they get hurt!

After ruling out a visual or structural problem, make a judgment about why your dog is crashing the jumps. Wait! Not so fast! You're copping out on this if you just assign him a label. That is useless in defining or changing behavior. Labeling him lazy, stubborn, excited, or careless will not help the situation. What can help is to pinpoint his way of going over the jumps, and

Figure 9-1. A solid foundation will help your dog recover rapidly from a mistake that causes him to crash a jump.

find the common denominator that results in crashing. Is he taking off way too soon, with a trajectory that apexes long before the jump and drops the dog into the jump on the descent? Is he crashing through on the uptake? Is he colliding with his chest or with his legs? Where is he looking when he crashes? How does he react when it happens? Read Paragraph 2 of Knocking Bars, above, for other specific questions, but above all, take notes about what you see going on when your dog crashes jumps. There is no substitute for reading the situation.

The healthy dog who habitually crashes jumps needs more strength, better judgment, more confidence, or increased motivation to attend to the job. Sometimes the handler becomes part of the problem by heaping additional stress on the dog. Beware! You can accidentally become a very powerful context cue^ for "crash anxiety," which can keep your dog crashing jumps under pressure long after his skills are up to par and the jumps themselves are no longer a problem.

Many dogs crash only spread jumps. This might seem to be a strength problem, but it generally is a judgment problem. Unlike oxers for horses, which often are as wide as they are high, the spread jumps our dogs see in competition require only a little more strength than regular jumps. (One notable exception is felt by tiny dogs, for whom the long jump is of major height, and oxers are as wide as their height.) Dogs need to recognize a spread from more than a stride away, since the PTS should be slightly earlier. The apex of the dog's trajectory should be halfway between the bars of a parallel spread and over the highest bar of an ascending spread. The dog who lands on top of the back bar of the triple spread has usually misread the jump completely and planned for an apex over the first (lowest) bar. He may read the height element properly, but takes off early enough to clear the low bar at that height; consequently, his trajectory descends into the highest bar at the back (Fig. 9-2). He needs to learn to apex over the back (highest) bar. See also Chapter 3, Level II, Step 7.

A quick-fix trick for dogs who were worked up to full spreads too quickly is the use of a take-off pole, a jump bar placed on the ground slightly in front of the jump for the purpose of defining the beginning of the jump effort. The pole is placed close enough to the jumps that the dog will choose to jump the two together. A dog who was trained through Levels I, II, and III would probably never need a take-off pole, because the lessons contained therein work to focus your dog on the top of the jump to improve his ability to judge height, and on a variety of presentations so that he can figure out his own PTS. The take-off pole is also called a ground line because it focuses the dog down and tells him where to take off. It can be useful for reschooling dogs who have the wrong idea about how to handle a certain type of jump, usually spreads or single-bar jumps. Practice first with low jumps, perhaps on leash. If your dog wants to take off extremely early in response to the ground line, add another pole or small jump before the ground pole so as to define a certain landing area before the take-off pole. A series of these low challenges in a jumping lane will soon calm your dog down. Praise each correct interpretation of landing and take-off areas.

Photo by Kathy Pepin

Figure 9-2. Apexing over the low bar is usually a judgement problem rather than a strength problem.

If your dog typically slams jump bars with his front feet when he crashes (Fig. 9-3), his PTS is either much too far back (he hits the bars on descent), much too close (he hits the bars on the ascent), or else he is resigned to barging through and is jumping too low to clear the jump from any spot. Your long-term reschooling efforts need to begin in Level I. In your focus sessions, set him up for success with easy jumps at first, and be sure to praise as his front feet clear the bars. Ignore what the back feet do until he has control of his front.

If your dog crashes jumps on the ascent due to taking off too late, and if he is strong enough to jump properly, you can use a take-off pole to encourage your dog to take off earlier. Start with the pole close to the jump and gradually move it further away from the jump. This is the best use of a take-off pole. Move it gradually enough that the dog doesn't choose to step between the pole and the jump.

Separate quick-fix tricks should consist of low jumps, unevenly spaced, in a lane, to let him rework his PTS. Somewhere along the way his education got rushed and he lost his comfort zone. Or perhaps he was trained to take off at a certain point and never found or expanded a comfort zone for himself. He needs to learn how to feel smart about jumping, and he also needs to develop a feel for his body (Chapter 5) and a good eye for assessing jumps (Chapter 3, Levels I and II). He needs to start over.

Photo by Kathy Pepin

Figure 9-3. This dog has just knocked the bar with his chest. The 30" jump height in USDAA agility requires that dogs have an extra measure of fitness and be well-schooled in judging the correct take-off spot.

There is a tiny percentage of dogs, usually agility performers, who become so intent on the next job that their minds leave their bodies behind to flounder over the jump at hand, which at that moment is inconsequential to them, merely in the way of the next obstacle — the one on which the dog is concentrating. The dog, we assume, is in no way deterred or put off by the crash. It's a big assumption, but it does seem to be so in a very few cases. Don't make this diagnosis without studying your video! For these dogs, the handler could effectively respond to crashes with the use of negative punishment, (i.e., the discouraging of a behavior by immediately removing a pleasurable stimulus; in this case, the opportunity to continue). In this context, the handler would immediately remove the dog from the ring when he crashes a jump.

When using negative punishment^, the message will be much clearer to the dog if the action is swift and NOT accompanied by verbal or physical garbage. Though you feel like telling him what you think of his carelessness, you are only clouding the message that the crash caused the end of the game.

From the dog's perspective it suddenly seems that you, not the crash, are the problem. That will hurt your future teamwork. You are not likely to convince this supercharged dog that he is the problem.

Also keep in mind that any punishment, including negative punishment, can only work if the dog understands at that moment how to fix the problem. If you've ever been too excited or distracted to remember something which you should know, would an ear pinch make you less nervous in the future? A dog who has come to accept crashing jumps as a solution to a pressure situation does not necessarily know what else to do at that moment. Negative punishment can be effective for those few dogs who desperately want to do everything at once, but it also requires reschooling to teach the dog an alternative way of handling himself. Positive punishment^ (i.e., yelling at the dog or otherwise adding a noxious stimulus to the soup) may seem to work by temporarily sobering the dog, but only makes him more nervous next time if he doesn't know how to control himself. Handler control is different from the dog's own self-control. Negative punishment can teach self-control.

Popping Jumps

The dog stops and hesitates briefly in front of the jump, then springs over, clearing the full height from a standstill. The crowd loves it. "What a talented jumper!" they exclaim. Well, maybe yes, and maybe no, but popping the jumps is not a habit to admire. Popping represents a lack of planning ahead for the jump, resulting in extra strain and much wasted time. A dog with strength to burn can get away with it physically, but at best it shows a lack of communication and teamwork.

At worst, popping jumps is a very serious resistance problem, often accompanied by stutter-stepping and stress. The dog is afraid of the job, doesn't want to jump, and puts off the decision for as long as possible without actually quitting (see Refusing Jumps). If a review of Chapter 3, Levels I and II shows no hole in the dog's foundation, or if onset is sudden in a trained dog, then a physical problem is most likely to blame. If the foundation is lacking, the work of reschooling begins all the way back at the beginning, at "A is for Attitude."

The quick-fix trick for popping full-height jumps is to ask for an earlier, smoother take-off. You can inspire this by spacing low jumps amply in a jumping lane (as in Chapter 3, Level I, Step 2, with some added height) and encouraging your dog to jump them on the run. Be enthusiastic and generous. Earlier take-offs come with speed and confidence. As your dog's comfort zone increases, he learns to trust his body, vary his strides, and enjoy his strength. It's a pretty process. Of course, vary your spacings all the time, but keep them extra roomy until your dog is relaxed and stretching out. Vary the heights also, but raise the average height of your lane very gradually.

Overjumping

See Chapter 3, Level III, Step 5 for more about this. The dog doesn't want any trouble with the jump and isn't sure how to read it, so he puts out much more effort than required and clears the jump with many extra inches to spare (Fig. 9-4). Over-jumping is a problem because it is harder on the dog's body (see Chapter 5), it wastes time and effort, and it is usually accompanied by stress. Suspect one of the following culprits:

1. A physical problem, usually vision. Is your dog as good at catching the ball as he used to be? Are the eyes of your middle-aged dog starting to show a blue haze? (This is a sign that the dog is not as good at focusing up close as he used to be. Those of you over 40 know what we mean.) Are the whites of your dog's eyes clean and white, or are they red and irritated? (If you have a droopy-lidded dog who always has bloodshot eyes, check the whites at the top of the eyeball. If it's not white up there, you have a problem.)

2. An inefficient jumping style. The dog learned to jump higher rather than to find a more efficient style. This is a training problem, usually attributable to working too quickly up to full height. Dogs with a fairly cobby^ build are most susceptible. That is the case with Julie's Springer, Arrow. Heavy-boned and cobby, he was jumping full height and more by 10 months of age. In 1990, at 12 months old, he became the youngest dog to earn a USDAA agility title. He overjumps in order to compensate for an early take-off and a loose tuck position. Even with a weight:height ratio of 2.0, he has had extensive shoulder problems, beginning at age four years. The rush to be "first" and "youngest" generally takes a heavy long-term toll on your dog. Ask Julie: she'll never do it quick and dirty again.

Correcting this kind of overjumping depends on reprogramming the dog's jumping style, which gets more difficult the longer he's been jumping that way. Since overjumping usually avoids knocking bars, most of us spend our training efforts on other problems. But starting over with this dog can improve his efficiency. Although Arrow reverts to poor form in competition, he can also demonstrate an efficient, full stretch style. He had been overjumping for four years when he was reschooled. As for a quick-fix trick, video analysis is necessary to assess whether the dog is taking off too soon and over-jumping just for insurance since he'll be descending over the jump. If that is the case, use varied claustrophobic jumping lanes or experiment with take-off poles to help your dog time his jumps better.

If his rear leg position is the culprit, you could use a jump circle or straddle the jump to ask for a tighter tuck.

3. A dog who was ritual trained rather than concept trained, who thinks that all jumps are to be jumped this way. In other words, the dog doesn't really assess the height of the jump; he just throws his body over it the only way he knows how.

Photo by Lewis Hizer

Figure 9-4. This dog is jumping much higher than is necessary to clear this jump which is much lower than her competition height.

You would expect this to be a problem resistant to reform, but even dogs who have been jumping needlessly high for years seem to be happy to change when they are started over from scratch. They act as if they are relieved to understand the job and are pleased to discover their powers of observation. If the dog also displays an awkward jumping position, then you have more work to do, and you should separate the two problems in your focus sessions. As for quick-fix tricks, it's fun to set up amply-spaced lanes of low jumps, as many in a row as you can. Even if you forget to praise each low trajectory, the dog will figure this out. After a short time, the trajectories at the end of the lane will be much lower than those at the beginning. In separate focus sessions, you could reinforce an outstretched neck rather than an upright head carriage, or a more efficient take-off spot, or a tighter tuck, if necessary, to help your dog improve his style.

Refusing Jumps

Refusing is often due to a physical problem but is always a confidence problem. The dogs who "just say no" are really trying to say, "I can't." The vast majority of handlers assume their dogs are saying, "I won't." Force can sometimes get the job done, but it does lasting damage to trust and enthusiasm, not to mention to the body if the dog is hurting.

A dog who is simply forced to jump when he refuses seldom progresses to smooth sailing as a result; stutter-stepping, popping jumps, and knock-downs are more likely. That alone speaks in favor of patience and reschooling rather than punishment to solve this problem. It is extremely important information for you if your dog refuses. Stop what you are doing and find out why. Go back to Chapter 3, Level I. This is one of those prime areas where shortcuts now mean gremlins later.

Stutter-stepping

It's sad to see a dog take some quick, tiny steps before launching his body over a jump. The dog has forfeited his momentum and his rhythm, both of which would have made the job easier. Stutter-stepping is always a confidence problem, so punishment is never appropriate. If the problem comes on suddenly in a trained dog, you can bet your allowance that the root of the problem is physical (read pain). It's that common. Consider everything from weight:height ratio to vision to structure to injury as possible causes. You are trifling with his long-term soundness if you keep making him jump this way.

If your dog started stutter-stepping when jumps were raised and has done so ever since, you know we're going to suggest lowering the jumps significantly and teaching all sorts of complicated skills of judgment, stride adjustment, and plain old confidence-building before raising them again. See especially Chapter 3, Level II. It would be nice to pinpoint what element of difficulty is especially troubling your dog. You may be able to take a good guess by reading Levels I and II to find a skill he may be missing. Other than raising to regulation height too rapidly, the hole in his jumping psyche is likely to be a lack of experience with unevenly spaced jumps. He should begin with Level I, which hopefully he can work through quickly and happily, and then start enjoying Level II.

The Five Most Common Training Errors in the Education of Canine Jumpers

We don't often make lists of 'wrong' things, because it tends to stick you with bad images. Good images are more helpful in teaching you what to do. But we want you to know these five mistakes by heart, because you will meet them everywhere. They will be offered to you as solutions to your jumping problems. We want you to recognize them when you see them and to know them for what they are: poor training ideas and shortcuts.

1. **Pulling up on the leash** as the dog goes over the jump. Unhelpful to say the least, it only throws him off balance and makes him apprehensive. To become a good jumper, your dog needs to round his spine and reach forward with his head and neck. Pulling up on the leash hollows his back and raises his head and neck, making it hard for him to find the ground, let alone find his natural rhythm. Let him explore jumping as in Chapter 3, on a loose leash, and then set up free-jumping series that allow him to learn to use his body efficiently and comfortably. Take the time to let him find and expand his comfort zone.

2. **Aways working at the same height.** Good jumping is a concept game, not a ritual game. Keep your jump heights varied, even when low, to keep your dog alert and more resourceful. Make your dog a scopey jumper. Many people who say their dogs are bored are really guilty of not varying the variables enough to keep the work interesting. Smart jumpers stay alert because they expect variation.

3. **Punishment.** Yelling at errors, rapping the feet as the dog jumps, grabbing the scruff if he tries to quit. All are quick and dirty fixes that sap the dog's confidence and produce stress. Ask yourself, "What's it like being trained by me?" Jumping problems can be fixed by pleasant means; see if you can turn away from what you don't want and turn toward what you do want. It takes more analysis from you and requires more patience, but it's extremely satisfying and effective to go back and build the skills your dog lacks. Stop calling your shortcuts by any other name. Stop thinking, "How can I make him do what I want?" and start thinking, "How can I make him want what I want?"

4. **Setting higher jumps because your dog hits lower jumps.** Don't do this! It's dangerous because your dog may be injured, and it will not improve his confidence. Teach your dog to recognize and jump what is actually there, no more, no less; he'll last longer and be a smarter partner that way. See Knocking Bars for some suggestions on identifying the details of your problem and setting up focus sessions to improve those details.

5. **Blaming your dog's jumping problems on your dog.** Stubborn? Lazy? Bored? How we hate those labels! How about badly trained? Weak

foundation? Shut down? Please look for physical problems, and read up on learning and motivation. Dogs aren't so different from us as you might think. For example, bored is only unmotivated. Many school children are instantly bored when it's time for math. They glaze over and daydream, they choose not to participate. That does not mean that they understand the work! "He's bored" is not a compliment to the teacher. You have the opportunity to attune your teaching to one dog at a time, to motivate him in sync with his own learning style. The problems and solutions belong to both of you together.

Jumping Problems — Recap

Your observational skills are important. It's never "just a phase" if your dog seems to lose his enjoyment for jumping. Somewhere along the line you have made a training error that has caught up to you (we all make these; we just don't always admit them). Rekindle your dog's enthusiasm and confidence before continuing further. Go back and polish the skills you may have rushed. Look for a physical problem like an on-again, off-again tendon injury, or a medical one, like infected anal glands, deep ear infections, eye infections, or thyroid dysfunction. Julie's Arrow had all five of these problems at once and competed badly for months before diagnosis!

If it's hard for you to learn from your mistakes, take heart: we have hundreds of our own for you to choose from and, because we're always training several dogs ourselves, we are guaranteed to continue making interesting mistakes and sharing them. Every dog is different. Everyone misses the boat and sets off on a wrong course with this or that problem. Sometimes you need a new perspective. Sometimes you need time off. In any case, you take your best guess at a problem and begin piecing together a solution. If you keep the communication lines open both ways and keep your priorities straight, you can solve your problem. Jumping is only jumping, after all, but the big picture is bettering our understanding, analytical skills, effectiveness, and interactive skills — now that can change the world!

NOTES

NOTES

Appendix A -
Glossary

AAC — Agility Association of Canada. Formerly ADAC, the association changed its name to facilitate translation to French. It is a non-profit club run strictly by volunteers. AAC offers both individual and club memberships. Sanctioned trials are open to registered dogs, and any dog may be registered. AAC rules are a combination of those of the USDAA and of the British Agility Club (where it all began). Jump heights are high.

AKC — American Kennel Club. The AKC is a club of clubs; membership is not open to individuals. It is technically non-profit, but derives a huge income from the registration of dogs from approximately 140 recognized breeds. The AKC sanctions competitions for these breeds in many sports including obedience, where jump heights are $1\frac{1}{4}$ times the dog's height at the withers (with some exceptions). The AKC has also introduced an agility program, which fills a welcome niche between the more structured UKC and the more difficult USDAA programs. Jump heights are moderate.

CKC — Canadian Kennel Club. The CKC is a club of individuals; membership is not open to clubs. It operates much like the AKC. The CKC recognizes hundreds of different breeds and sanctions competitions for its registered dogs, including obedience but not agility or flyball. Obedience jump heights are equal to the height of the dog at the withers.

Cobby — Approximately equal in body length and body height. Length is measured from the point of the shoulder to the point of the buttocks (the backmost point of the pelvic bone — see Fig. 1-10). Height is measured from the ground to the top of the shoulder blades (see Fig. 1-6). Cobby dogs are also called "square." Many breed standards prefer a cobby specimen, but it does not make for fluid jumping. A cobby body has a short back with minimal spinal flexion. The hind legs tend to interfere with the front if the dog is well angulated (see Fig. 1-11).

Context cue — A stimulus that triggers a certain behavior which has become associated with it, consciously or unconsciously. A very common problem among competition dogs who have been over-stressed is that context cues of the competition scene (the judge, the handler's nervousness, the ring gates, the loudspeaker, certain command words, etc.) conjure up feelings of insecurity long after the dog's performance problem itself (perhaps a jumping problem) has been solved at home. This is the basis of competition-specific stress and "ring-wise" dogs. It is important that the process of solving jumping problems gradually include every possible context cue for the problem so each one may become associated with new behavior and good feelings.

Crossing — Changing sides with the dog while running a sequence or course. Crossing behind means switching sides after sending the dog ahead, and crossing in front refers to switching sides before the dog reaches that spot on the line of travel. Used primarily for

169

agility, but also for teaching mental and physical flexibility, informal attention, surprise recalls, etc.

Cross-training — Participating in different sports in order to develop different strengths. The second sport is often chosen for its direct bearing on an aspect of the primary sport, but this is not necessarily the case. Sometimes the goal is simply to improve physical ability and confidence overall. Thus hiking in the woods is certainly wonderful cross-training for competition jumping, but getting out and meeting new people will be equally helpful for shy dogs.

Front — In obedience competition, this is a position required during the recall. The dog must come directly to the handler and sit squarely in front of him, facing his legs, and positioned within arm's reach, preferably looking up at the handler's face.

Lead leg — The last front leg to touch down during each canter stride. The lead leg lands forward of the other legs. During turns, the lead leg twists in the direction of the turn, proportionate to the severity of the turn (dogs have this dexterity more than horses — see Ch. 1). When turning, the dog (or horse) should always be cantering on the inside lead, that is, the leg to the inside of the bend should be the furthest forward in each stride. Cantering on the outside lead bends the body away from the direction of the turn and throws the animal out of balance. Cross-cantering refers to being on conflicting leads, the left lead with the front legs and the right lead with the rear legs or vice versa. This is discouraged in horses but regularly seen in dogs.

NADAC — North American Dog Agility Council. A non-profit corporation with membership open to individuals and clubs. Dogs must be registered to compete in sanctioned trials, and any dog may be registered. Rules are loosely based on international standards. Course designs are generally spacious and fluid, and jump heights are moderate.

North American Flyball Association (NAFA) — A non-profit organization very active in both the U.S. and Canada. Membership is open to individuals and clubs. NAFA sponsors tournaments and sanctions flyball competitions. The sport is open to all dogs. Jump heights are very low.

Negative punishment — The discouraging of a behavior by removing a desired stimulus (or removing the dog from his desired stimulus) as an immediate consequence of that unwanted behavior. To cement the connection between the unwanted behavior and the removal of the stimulus, the consequence must be immediate and not confused by extraneous additional stimuli (like yelling or laughing).

Plastic genetic make-up — Because of the ease with which his genetic make-up can be altered through breeding, the dog, *Canis familiaris*, is a perfect example of an animal species whose evolution can be influenced by human interference. The quintessential mongrel dog, a more "natural" canid, is about 30 pounds, brown in color, short haired, with a curled tail. But, in an amazingly short time by evolutionary standards, humans have splintered *Canis familiaris* into hundreds of different shapes and characteristics, temperaments and drives, with all sorts of mutually exclusive genetic traits. The dog is a very accommodating animal, genetically as well as environmentally.

Positive punishment — What's positive about punishment? In the scientific sense, "positive" refers only to the fact that a stimulus is added rather than removed. In the scientific sense, "punishment" decreases the likelihood that a behavior will recur. For simplicity, we just call this process "discouraging the behavior." The scientific definition reminds us that an unpleasant consequence must be immediate in order to be an effective punisher, for otherwise it might not be associated with the behavior we want to discourage. As mentioned elsewhere in the text, mistimed positive punishment is more likely to do harm than mistimed positive reinforcement.

Positive reinforcer — As above, "positive" only means a stimulus is added. A reinforcer is an incentive, a desired stimulus, which will increase the likelihood that a behavior will recur. We simply call this "encouraging the behavior." Again, in order for a consequence to be a positive reinforcer, it must be associated with the behavior we want to encourage.

PTS — Preferred take-off spot. This is the area from which the dog prefers to take off when lifting himself over a jump. Commensurate with the dog's talent and experience, the PTS will be adjusted from one jumping situation to another depending on the parameters of the task. We want our dogs to find their own PTS as part of developing ability and becoming concept jumpers rather than ritual jumpers. We do this by making the decision interesting but not threatening from the very beginning, by letting the dog become comfortable with his body and his mind, and by building a solid foundation.

Roadwork — A specific kind of exercise in which the dogs maintains a rhythmic, extended trot over gradually longer distances. Roadwork builds endurance along with muscle strength and bone density. The rule of thumb is known as LSD (long, slow distance). Other variations which can strengthen specific body parts include trotting uphill, in soft sand, or for short distance on hard roads. Roadwork outside is far superior to treadmill work because of the contribution of many soft-tissue support structures involved in maintaining balance on the ground, which is never as perfect or predictable as a treadmill. Roadwork is also more interesting, so is a better mental preparation for sports.

Scopey — This is a term borrowed from the horse world. Horsemen define the term differently, but they usually agree which horse has more scope. An athlete's scope is an informal measure of this athletic potential, and it's more than physical fitness. A scopey dog is a combination of confidence, work ethic, readiness, common sense, body awareness, and physical athleticism. Concept jumping requires scope, and power jumpers are very scopey.

First Jump Set-up Distance — This is the distance from the dog to the jump on start-up. This distance is decided by the handler when he sets his dog up, so it warrants some experimentation to discover what sort of space is most advantageous to the dog. Generally speaking, the more strides your dog can take to the jump the better, but some dogs jump more carefully and accurately when they have little room to spare and thus don't take off too early. There is no substitute for allowing your dog to try different set-up distances and watching how he decides to use his body from various spots.

Soft tissue — It's not that these important support elements are soft, it's just that they're softer than bones. Most important to jumping, soft tissues include tendons and ligaments, which attach muscle to bone and bone to bone, respectively. Strains and tears to these fibers can sometimes damage the canine athlete more than a broken bone. If only torn ligaments and strained tendons could be put in a cast and permanently healed! With or without surgery, the treatment is extended rest (usually a few months), and then a high likelihood of recurrence when extensive demands are made again, even if the injured area is gradually muscled up. Surely some animals are predisposed to suffer soft-tissue injuries, but the risk is much smaller if your dog is kept lean and strong.

Stack — This refers to having the dog assume a certain stance, with his four pasterns perpendicular to the ground, his neck rather high, his weight shifted slightly forward, and his chin level. This is the pose used to evaluate a dog's structure in the dog show conformation ring, for the same reason we are using it in this book: it allows an objective and relative evaluation of the interfitting of the dog's skeleton. As mentioned, the sling-like rather than fused fit of canine shoulders make it impossible to evaluate the front accurately without some standard stance. The stack position is often assumed by dogs when they are on alert, because they are drawn up to their full height and their weight is balanced evenly, poised for action. That sums up the balance and grace we like to see in a canine athlete.

Stimulus — Any situation or event (internal or external) which is capable of inciting a response. (The perceiving of the stimulus constitutes a response in the strictest sense, but in this book we are speaking more generally.) Thus, the far-off sound which your dog perceives is a stimulus for him, but not for you if you are unable to hear it. However, your dog's attending to that sound while you want his attention may be a strong stimulus for you.

UKC — United Kennel Club. A tax-paying business, not non-profit, its members are clubs, not individuals. UKC recognizes about 212 breeds, and also sponsors performance events open to any dog. Obedience jump heights are equal to the height of the dog at the withers. UKC has also taken over the administration of the agility program formerly known as NCDA, a popular downscaled and more structured version of agility designed so that any dog can compete.

USDAA — United States Dog Agility Association. A tax-paying business, not non-profit. Membership is open to individuals and groups. Dogs must be registered to compete in sanctioned trials, and any dog may be registered. USDAA rules loosely follow international standards based on those of the British Agility Club. USDAA offers the most challenging agility tests among the U.S. versions of the sport. Jump heights are high.

Wings — Wings are the pet name given to the decorative side supports found on many jumps in the agility ring. They constitute a separate element of difficulty; some are even shaped and painted like dogs. We advise introducing wings into jumping practice no later than Level II. It's also smart to change the look of your wings unpredictably by hanging odd materials on them. You can simulate wings by standing extraneous materials next to your plain jump stanchions, too; anything from barrels to step ladders to hay bales. Many an otherwise fine jumper has been fooled in agility by his misinterpretation of a wing. Your dog should always look for the bars and not worry about wings.

Appendix B -
Where To Call

The following organizations provide information on conditions that can affect performance and supply lists of veterinarians that can perform appropriate health checks.

Hip Dysplasia

Orthopedic Foundation for Animals
2300 Nifong Blvd.
Columbia, MO 65201
(314) 442-0418

PennHip
c/o International Canine Genetics
271 Great Valley Pkwy.
Malvern, PA 19355
(800) 248-8099

Elbow Dysplasia

Orthopedic Foundation for Animals, address above

Eye Disorders

Canine Eye Registration Foundation
1235 SCC-A
Purdue University
W. Lafayette, IN 47907-1235
(317) 494-8179

Cardiac Conditions

American College of Veterinary Internal Medicine (Cardiology)
7175 West Jefferson Ave., Suite 2125
Lakewood, CO 80235
(303) 980-7136

Appendix C -
Imperial-Metric Conversion Table

Inches	Cm.
1	2.5
2	5
3	7.5
4	10
5	12.5
6	15
8	20
10	25
12	30
15	37.5
16	40
18	45
20	50
24	60
26	65
30	75
32	80

Feet	Meters
1	0.3
2.5	0.75
3	0.9
5	1.5
6	1.8
7.5	2.3
8	2.4
9	2.7
10	3.0
12	3.6
14	4.2
15	4.5
16	4.8
18	5.4
20	6.0
24	7.2
30	9.0
32	9.6
35	10.5
40	12.0
50	15.0

Miles	Km.
0.04	0.06
0.62	1.0
1	1.6
4	6.4
6	.96
8	12.8
10	16.0
12	19.2

Lbs.	Kg.
1	0.45
5	2.3
10	4.6
15	6.8
20	9.1
30	13.6
40	18.2

Yards	Meters
1	0.9
2	1.8
3	2.7
4	3.6
5	4.5
10	9
11	9.9

Index